VEGETABLE AND HERB
Gardening

pil

Publications International, Ltd.

Let's get social!
@Publications_International
@PublicationsInternational
www.pilbooks.com

CONTENTS

CHAPTER 1: PLANNING YOUR GARDEN

Whether you like to cook or simply like to eat, a vegetable and herb garden can be the perfect upgrade to your home. You can start growing vegetables early in spring and keep planting throughout the growing season so that something fresh and tasty is always ready to harvest.

Spring is the time to enjoy lettuce, spinach, and asparagus. In summer, tomatoes, peppers, and squash are ripe for the picking. In fall, salad fixings appear in the form of radishes, carrots, and lettuce.

But easy access to flavorful produce is just one benefit of a vegetable garden. Growing your own vegetables organically means fresh, nutrient-rich, pesticide-free produce without the high prices of organically grown produce from the grocery store.

WHAT TO GROW

First, you must decide which vegetables and herbs to grow. Think about which produce you and your family enjoy. Leafing through the vegetable and herb profile chapters at the back of this book can help ensure you don't forget any favorites. Before you finalize your list, though, you need to consider whether the vegetables you've chosen will have enough time to produce a crop during your area's growing season. For example, winter squash and some other vegetables need a relatively long time to mature and may not be suitable if your area has a short growing season.

THE GROWING SEASON

The growing season is the number of days between the last frost in spring and the first of the fall. This is the amount of time any vegetables you plant in your garden will have to go from seed (or transplant) to maturity and produce a crop. (In parts of the country that rarely have frost, the dry season serves as "winter," or the end of the growing season.)

To find out how long your growing season is and when it typically begins and ends, call your county cooperative extension (get the number online or from the reference librarian of your local library). The average dates of last-spring and first-fall frosts for various areas of the country are also widely available on the Internet; search for "last spring frost [your town]" and "first fall frost [your town]," and count the days between them to get the length of the season.

Then, to ensure that your growing season will be long enough for your chosen vegetables and herbs, check the "days to maturity" listed in the seed catalog or on the seed packet for each. (The vegetable and herb profile chapters also provide maturity information.) This number indicates the average number of days needed from germination or transplanting (depending on how the vegetable is typically grown) to harvest. The days-to-maturity must fit comfortably within the number of frost-free days in your region.

If your growing season is a bit tight for a particular variety, see if there's a variety that matures in fewer days.

SELECTING VARIETIES

Growing your own vegetables and herbs opens a whole world of choices. Instead of planting just any tomato, for example, you can select from different sizes, colors, and features: big to plum-size to cherry ones; red, green, yellow, orange, or even striped ones; and ones with or without seeds or with or without resistance to certain diseases. Such versions of a specific plant, which differ from one another in minor ways, are called varieties. The differences may be obvious, such as in the color, size, or shape of the fruit, or subtler, such as improved disease resistance, better flavor, or compact growth. A hybrid is specifically bred for success; it is a cross between two parent plants that have been selected and bred for a certain desirable characteristic, such as the size of their fruit or their ability to resist disease.

You'll find many varieties described in the vegetable and herb profile chapters. You can also learn about varieties from seed catalogs or your local cooperative extension. A good way to choose from among the many varieties, especially for the new gardener, is to look for those designated All-America Selections (AAS). AAS is a nonprofit organization that uses a network of skilled, impartial gardeners all over the United States to test and judge new seed varieties and select and promote those that reliably show superior garden performance.

SKETCH OUT A PLAN

Before you plant, draw up a simple plan for your garden, and arrange plantings to make the most of available space. Plan to train sprawling, vining vegetables like cucumbers up trellises or fencing to free up valuable planting ground. Place

taller plants or trellised vines in the north or northeast portion of the garden, so they won't shade other plants. And situate crops that come back year after year, such as asparagus or strawberries, in a corner, where they won't interfere with future tilling or garden maintenance.

In smaller gardens, it's more efficient to plant in one or two wide rows or in four- to five-foot-wide beds than in the traditional configuration of multiple narrow (single-plant-wide) rows separated by wide soil paths, as is often recommended on seed packets. You will be able to reach the center of the row or bed comfortably from either side, without wasting space on paths.

WHEN TO PLANT

Maximizing your garden's yield means knowing which plants do well in the cool of spring, after the soil has thawed and dried out enough to be worked, and which require weeks in the warm air and warm soil of summer to thrive and produce plentiful crops.

EARLY, COOL-SEASON VEGETABLES

Very hardy vegetables, such as radishes and peas, can be planted in the garden four to six weeks before the average date of the last spring frost. Broccoli, brussels sprouts, and other members of the cabbage family, or "cole crops," are also quite tolerant of cold and can be planted very early in the season.

A few weeks later, you can add other cool-season vegetables, including lettuce, onions, and potatoes. These plants can handle some cold and frost and can be planted two to three weeks before the average date of the last spring frost. After the average last-spring-frost date, when the soil is still fairly cool, you can plant beets and carrots.

Cool-season vegetables mature quickly. So, you can keep your early harvest going by planting a second round of radishes, lettuce, peas, spinach, or other early vegetables about two weeks after you plant the first. They will still have time to mature before the weather gets too hot for them to thrive.

After you harvest your early cool-season crops, replant the space with warm-season vegetables, and when they've been harvested, plant another round of cool-season vegetables for the fall. Through "succession planting," you'll make the most of your space, and your garden will produce all season long.

WHEN TO PLANT

Very early (as soon as soil can be worked; 4 to 6 weeks before average date of last spring frost)

Early (1 to 2 weeks before average date of last spring frost)

Soon after date of last spring frost

Once soil warms (2 to 3 weeks after average date of last spring frost)

About 2 months before average date of first fall frost

WHAT TO PLANT

Broccoli; brussels sprouts, and other "cole crops" of the cabbage family; peas; radishes

Asparagus; Chinese greens; lettuce and other salad greens; onion sets (bulbs); potatoes; spinach, strawberries

Beets; carrots

Beans; corn; cucumbers; melons; okra; peppers; pumpkins; squash; sweet potatoes; tomatoes; zucchini

Broccoli; kohlrabi and other "cole crops" in the cabbage family; garlic; lettuce; spinach

WARM-SEASON VEGETABLES

Many popular garden crops, including beans, cucumbers, corn, peppers, tomatoes, and squash, don't like cold. You'll need to wait until the air and soil are warm, about two to three weeks after the average date of the last spring frost, to plant them.

You should also be ready to protect your warm-season vegetables from a surprise frost or cold snap in spring or fall:

- In a pinch, an old bedsheet or tablecloth will protect your plants against a light frost. Cover the plants the night a frost is predicted (use garden stakes to tent the cloth over fragile plants), and uncover them the following morning.
- If cold is forecast, cover your plants with heavy-duty floating row covers made of spun polyester. Available from garden centers and catalogs, they can protect plants from frosts and light freezes in spring and fall. You can leave them in place for longer periods, because light and rain penetrate the fabric.
- Use special water-filled tepees around tomatoes and other tender vegetables for protection from the cold. Garden centers and catalogs sell inexpensive plastic sheets of connected tubes that, when filled with water, form self-supporting walls around seedlings. The clear walls allow sun to penetrate to the plant, and the solar-heated water stays warm into the night.

To increase your garden's yield even more, consider planting short-term, cool water crops, such as radishes and lettuce, between warm-weather plants that take longer to mature, such as tomatoes and peppers. By the time the tomatoes and peppers need the space, you'll have harvested the radishes and lettuce.

THE FALL GARDEN

In mid- to late summer—about eight weeks before the average date of the first fall frost—you can plant another round of cool-season vegetables. Choose crops for this fall planting that will not only continue to thrive as the temperature begins to drop but will have enough time to produce a harvest before it gets too cold even for them. Check the number of "days to maturity" listed in the catalog or on the seed packet to be sure. Good bets include fast-maturing, cool-season cabbage-family members.

To stretch your garden's yield for the growing season even further, consider a cold frame, which looks and acts like a little flat-topped greenhouse for your plants. Heated for free by the sun, a cold frame makes it possible to grow lettuce earlier in spring as well as later in fall. The frame is typically rectangular and about 18 inches tall, made of wood, and covered with clear plastic that allows sunlight to penetrate and heat the air within the frame and keeps that warmed air from escaping. The top is hinged so you can prop it open to water and tend the plants and keep the inside temperature from rising too high on mild, sunny days. Plant lettuce seeds or seedlings in the frame, and keep the lid shut to hold in heat.

Keeping a record or diary will help you learn what works best in your garden. For each vegetable variety, note the date(s) you planted it; any problems with weeds, insects, or rainfall; whether the harvest was sufficient, too much, or not enough; and how much you liked the variety. Use this information to help you plan next year's garden.

CHAPTER 2: BUILDING A GREAT FOUNDATION

On the housekeeping and laundry battlefields, dirt is the enemy. When it comes to gardening, though, nothing could be further from the truth. In the hands of a knowing gardener, dirt is transformed into soil, a complex and beautiful blend of animal, vegetable, and mineral material. Good soil is the bedrock of a great vegetable garden.

The loose, dark earth that fosters fabulous gardens rarely occurs naturally. It is created by gardeners who improve their native soil. Soil may be amended with sand to make it looser and drier, for example, or with clay to make it moister and firmer. It's also typically fed plentiful doses of organic material—compost, dried leaves, ground-up twigs, rotted livestock manure, old lawn clippings—to better nourish plant growth. And it's turned or tilled with care to give plant roots plenty of room to roam.

To begin creating that kind of quality foundation for your own vegetable-growing endeavors, start by choosing a good location for your garden.

PICK YOUR PLOT WITH CARE

It's generally best to situate your garden in a sunny spot, one that gets at least eight hours of direct sunlight daily. Vegetables grown for their fruit, such as tomatoes and peppers, need a minimum six to eight hours of direct light each day. If they get less, the plants may never produce flowers or fruit, even though they may look green and healthy.

Of course, there are some vegetables—root crops such as carrots and radishes, for example—that do fine in partial shade; they are good candidates for areas of your yard that might not get quite as much direct sunlight. And crops such as salad greens (lettuce and spinach) not only do well in partial shade, they may wilt if given full sun during the height of summer. But you needn't create a separate, shady garden if you want to grow them. They'll be happy in your sunny plot if they're planted in the shade of larger plants or if they're grown early in the season, when the air and soil are cooler and the sun's rays are not as strong.

Select an open area for your garden, away from trees and large shrubs. Not only are they likely to throw shade on your sun-loving vegetables, their roots will make it harder for you to dig and cultivate the soil. Their roots will also compete with your vegetables for water and nutrients. Be sure your garden site is well drained, too, rather than in a low area where water pools after a rain. And keep your garden near your kitchen if you can, so you'll be able to pop out quickly to pick fresh produce at the peak of ripeness as you prepare meals.

What size to make your garden plot depends on your interest in gardening and how much time you'll be able to devote to it. The larger the garden, the more time and work it will need. Unless you're already hooked on gardening, it's better to start small and let garden size increase as your gardening interest, experience, and confidence grow.

TURN IT OVER

Once you've chosen the location of your garden bed and decided on its size, you need to manually turn or rototill the soil thoroughly. For a small garden, you may be able to turn the soil over yourself using a spade or garden fork. Otherwise, rototilling is the fastest and easiest approach. You can rent a rototiller from a local home improvement or garden center and do the job yourself or hire someone to do it for you. Turn the soil twice (until a tiller or spade goes through it easily) when it's neither soggy nor bone dry.

If the area you've chosen is covered with grass, you can remove the sod first and then till the soil, or you can till without removing the grass and then pick out the clumps of turf after.

The job of stripping the sod before tilling is actually much easier than it sounds, and it'll save you from having to rake out clumps of grass after each round of tilling. The roots of lawn grass are shallow and thickly knitted together, so the sod will peel off in strips once you get it started.

To strip the sod by hand, slice all along the perimeter of your garden plot with a lawn-edging tool. Then, using a hoe, loosen and lift the edge of a section of sod about two feet wide. Pull the strip backward with the hoe, rolling it loosely like a rug as you work. If you encounter deep-rooted dandelions or other stubborn weeds, remove them with a hand trowel or pop them out with a skinny, forked tool sometimes called a "dandelion digger." Once you have removed the grass, till the entire plot length-wise. Then, till it across its width to thoroughly break up the soil.

To till without first pulling up the grass, begin by working down the length of the plot. Till adjacent or, if you're using a rototiller, slightly overlapping rows until you've turned over the entire plot. Rake out the clumps of grass and weeds with a short-pronged rake. Then, till the entire plot again, this time working across its width, until the soil is broken into reasonably small pieces. Finally, rake the plot again to remove any remaining weeds or clumps of grass.

In subsequent years, you can rototill the garden again or just use a spade or garden fork to turn the soil and incorporate another thick layer of organic matter before spring planting.

INVESTIGATE AND IMPROVE YOUR SOIL

Although your well-tilled soil may look pretty good at first glance, you need to get to know it on a deeper level and make whatever improvements are necessary to ensure it will be a good home for your vegetable plants.

The amounts of clay, silt, and sand in a soil determine its texture. Loam, the ideal garden soil, is a mixture of 20 percent clay, 40 percent silt, and 40 percent sand.

Test your soil by feel to judge its texture. Take a small handful of lightly moist soil from several inches below the surface, squeeze it into a ball, and watch the

results when you open your hand. Sandy soils, which can have a scratchy feel, will fall apart. Clay soils, which have a slick feel, will form a tight ball that's not easily broken up.

You can also check your soil's texture using a jar and water. This simple home test will give you important information. Just gather some soil from near the garden's surface as well as from a depth of about eight inches. Let it dry, pulverize it into fine granules, and mix it together well. Put one generous cup of soil and  1/4 teaspoon dishwasher detergent into a one-quart glass jar. Add enough water to fill the jar two-thirds full. Shake the jar for a minute, turning it upside down as needed to get all the soil off the bottom. Place the jar on a counter where it can sit undisturbed. After one minute, the sand particles in the jar will have settled into a layer at the bottom. Use a crayon or wax pencil to mark the height of the sand layer on the jar. Four hours later, mark the next level of settled particles, the silt layer. Over the next day or two, the clay will slowly settle out and allow you to take the final measurement. These measurements will tell you the relative percentages of sand, silt, and clay in your soil.

Soil that has a high percentage of sand (70 percent or more) tends to be well aerated and will be ready for planting earlier in spring. However, such sandy soil also tends to need more frequent watering and fertilizing than heavier soils. To improve sandy soil and keep it moist longer, till several inches of compost (partially decayed plant waste) and an inch or two of clay into the soil, then test the soil by making a ball. When the soil is improved, the ball will hold its shape but be easy to break apart.

Soil containing 35 percent or more clay retains more moisture, so it takes longer to dry out in spring, delaying planting. On the positive side, it will likely need less watering in summer. To improve clay soil and increase aeration, till in compost and coarse sand until a ball of the soil breaks up with a tap of your finger.

The best way to keep soil loose, light, and nutrient rich is to add a four- to six-inch-deep layer of compost or other organic matter and work it into the soil to a depth of 10 to 12 inches. The soil will become darker, moister, and spongier right before your eyes.

One you've mixed in the organic matter, try not to disturb the soil too much. Avoid additional tilling; it will only break up healthy soil clumps and speed the decay of organic matter. Instead of tilling, loosen rich soil before planting by turning the surface shallowly with a shovel and breaking large clumps apart with a smack from the back of the shovel. If your soil is still fairly loose after improvement, comb it with a hoe or cultivator before planting.

As long as the organic matter remains in the soil, the soil is likely to stay loose. But since organic matter slowly decays, you will have to continue to add more to maintain the desired soil texture.

SOURCES OF ORGANIC MATTER

Almost anything that began its life as a plant and doesn't contain pesky seeds can be a good source of organic matter for the garden, including:

- Compost
- Shredded fall leaves
- Livestock manure, composted and aged
- Straw
- Grass clippings
- Seedless annual weeds/plants
- Kitchen vegetable scraps
- Salt hay
- Peat moss
- Mushroom compost
- Agricultural remains such as peanut hulls or ground corncobs

HAVE THE SOIL TESTED

The next step in your soil-improvement program is to have the soil tested for nutrient levels. Call your local cooperative extension service and ask them how to get a soil testing kit. The kit will contain a soil collecting bag and instructions. Follow the directions precisely for accurate results. Your soil sample will be sent to a laboratory to identify any deficiencies in the nutrients needed for successful plant growth. Be sure to indicate that the samples came from a vegetable-garden plot.

The soil-test results will report the nutrient levels in your soil and specify which nutrients are lacking. They'll also note your soil's pH level and organic content, two important factors affecting soil fertility.

The results may come as a chart full of numbers, which can be a little intimidating at first. But if you look carefully for the following, you can begin to interpret these numbers:

- If the level of organic matter is under 5 percent, the garden needs some extra compost.
- Nutrients will be listed individually, possibly in parts per million. Sometimes, the report will include a rating—high, medium, or low—of how available those nutrients are in your soil. If an element comes in on the low side, you'll want to add a fertilizer that replaces what's lacking.
- Soil pH refers to the acidity of the soil. Ratings below seven indicate acidic soil. Soils rated six to seven are slightly acidic—considered the most fertile pH range. A rating greater than seven indicates alkaline, or base, soil. And a rating above eight means the soil is infertile.

The soil lab will consider the type of soil you have, the pH level, and the crops you intend to produce and will make a recommendation for pH adjustment. It will also recommend the amount and kind of fertilizer your garden needs. Follow the laboratory's recommendations as closely as possible during the first growing season. At your garden center, you'll find nutrients (available in various forms) for fertilizing/amending garden soil, including:

- Boron (manure, borax, chelated boron)
- Calcium (bonemeal, limestone, eggshells, wood ashes, oyster shells, chelated calcium)
- Copper (chelated copper)
- Iron (chelated iron, iron sulfate)
- Magnesium (Epsom salts, dolomitic limestone, chelated magnesium)
- Nitrogen (composted livestock manure, bat guano, chicken manure, fish emulsion, blood meal, kelp meal, cottonseed meal)
- Phosphorus (bonemeal, rock phosphate, super phosphate)
- Potassium (granite meal, sulfate of potash, greensand, wood ashes, seabird guano, shrimp shell meal)
- Sulfur (sulfur, iron sulfate, zinc sulfate)
- Zinc (zinc sulfate, chelated zinc)

ADJUSTING SOIL PH

The pH number of soil is important because it affects the availability of most of the essential nutrients required by plants. Fortunately, excessively acidic or alkaline soils can be treated to make them more moderate and productive.

Your soil report may advise you to raise the pH in your garden by adding a specific amount of lime to the soil. Ground dolomitic limestone is the best source to use and can be applied at any time of the year without harm to plants.

Conversely, your soil report may advise you to lower the pH of your soil by adding a recommended amount of a sulfur product. Ammonium sulfate is the product most commonly used.

When adding a lime or sulfur product, spread it evenly over your garden, and turn it into the soil.

CONSIDER DOUBLE-DIGGING

The average rototiller works only the top eight to ten inches of soil and won't break up compacted soil below. But a technique called double-digging will. If you want the ultimate in high-performance gardens—one that allows roots to grow deep into nutrient-rich soil—double-dig your garden plot instead of simply turning or rototilling the soil.

Double-digging requires some serious manual labor. If you have a bad back, a heart condition, or other health restriction, skip it or hire a professional landscaper to do it for you. If you're in good shape and choose to tackle it on your own, pace yourself and don't overdo it.

Start with soil that has had grass and all other vegetation removed. Beginning at one end of the garden, dig out a strip of soil a spade's length deep and a spade's width wide, and shovel it directly into a wheelbarrow. Then use your shovel to turn and break up the soil below the level you removed (this is likely to be the heaviest part of the job), or jab a garden fork into the hard lower soil and rock it back and forth until the soil breaks up (this latter approach may be easier). If your soil requires more organic matter, add it to the lower layer at this point.

Repeat this procedure on the adjacent strip of soil, but instead of dumping the top layer of soil into a wheelbarrow, dump it into the first trench and mix in additional organic matter and/or other amendments your soil needs. Loosen and amend (add organic matter to) the lower layer of the second strip as you did in the first strip. Then proceed to the third strip, and so forth, shifting the top layer of soil into the preceding trench and loosening and amending the soil in the lower layer. Fill the final strip with the soil from the wheelbarrow, and turn in some organic matter and/or other necessary amendments.

RAISED BEDS AND CONTAINERS

Sometimes, the native soil is simply too hard, rocky, poor, or wet for plants to grow well. Instead of struggling to change these miserable growing conditions, you can construct a great garden on top of them using raised beds or, easier still, opt for a versatile container garden.

The simplest way to make raised beds in a vegetable garden is to mound good soil into planting rows, with walking paths between them. Purchase and combine topsoil and organic compost, and use a short-toothed soil rake to shift the soil into mounded rows six to eight inches high, two to three feet wide, and up to ten feet long. The paths beside the plant-

ing rows will allow you to tend your plants without compressing the soil in the raised beds. Adding more organic matter to the raised beds and covering them with organic mulch throughout the growing season will keep the soil within them light and fluffy.

You can even opt for a permanent and decorative raised-bed garden by framing the mounds with walls that are four inches to four feet high and built of timbers, logs, rocks, or bricks. (Indeed, raised beds can make vegetable gardening accessible to individuals in wheelchairs and those with other physical limitations that make gardening at ground level impractical, uncomfortable, or impossible.) For these structures to last season after season, they need to be strong and secure, so don't hesitate to call in the pros to build (and even fill) the frames for you.

Another option to consider, whether you need an alternative to a traditional ground-level vegetable garden or simply want to expand your garden space, is growing vegetables in containers. Many vegetables—especially tomatoes, eggplants, peppers, cucumbers, and salad greens—flourish in containers. It's as easy as filling a large container (one that's at least ten inches across at the top) with potting soil and planting vegetable seeds or seedlings in it.

You can squeeze even more productivity out of limited space by planting lettuce and other low-growing greens around a tomato or pepper plant in a single container. Or add flowers to a container planted with vegetables: Try pairing pure white petunias with purple eggplants or yellow marigolds with cherry tomatoes, for example. If you are growing vegetables that need support, such as tomatoes or cucumbers, simply place their planters next to a trellis or fence.

The big advantage to gardening in containers is you won't have to do much, if any, weeding. But the soil in containers does dry out quickly, so you will have to water frequently, as often as once a day in hot, dry weather. To keep your container garden thriving, apply a water-soluble fertilizer every other week, or use a slow-release natural fertilizer.

USE THE RIGHT TOOLS

One sure way to make your gardening efforts more productive is to use the proper tools. Fortunately, you won't need many. Along with a sturdy wheelbarrow, these tools should suffice for your vegetable-garden jobs:

- Spade
- Garden fork
- Hoe
- Cultivator
- Short-toothed soil rake
- Hand trowel

Select tools that feel good in your hands and aren't too heavy or tall for you to use properly (and comfortably). If you have a smaller build, look for specially designed tools with smaller blades and shorter handles; they'll be easier to control than tools designed for someone much bigger.

Keep all of your tools together—and return them to their proper place after each use—so they'll be easy to find when needed. And be sure to store them covered to protect the wooden handles and metal parts from moisture.

If possible, keep a bucket of clean sand mixed with machine oil in the garage or shed to cure tools after each use. This is particularly helpful for rust-prone digging instruments such as spades, garden forks, and hoes. After use, rinse the tools with water, and dry them thoroughly. Then insert the metal end of each in the oil-sand mixture. The sand will scour off any stuck-on debris; the oil will coat the metal, retarding rust. When the blade of your spade or hoe begins to get dull and takes more effort to use, sharpen it with a sharpening stone just as you would a knife. Choosing and caring for your tools in this way will help ensure that they'll serve your gardening needs for many seasons to come.

CHAPTER 3: PLANTING, WATERING, AND FEEDING YOUR GARDEN

Once you've planned your garden and prepared a rich soil bed, it's time to begin planting. The easiest and least expensive way to grow most vegetables is to sow seed directly into your garden. In some circumstances, however, transplanting seedlings into the garden may be more appropriate.

SOWING SEEDS IN THE GARDEN

Since even the largest nurseries must limit the plants they stock, starting from seed will give you the widest selection of vegetable varieties. You can try almost any variety of vegetable that catches your eye in a seed catalog, as long as your growing season suits its needs. And for the price of a single transplant from a nursery, you can grow many plants from seed. A single packet of tomato seeds, for example, may contain several dozen seeds. Plant the seeds according to the directions on the packet. Eggplant and peppers can be slow to germinate, but nearly all other vegetables will sprout within a few days of being sown in the garden. Keep the soil moist until the seeds sprout. Once the plants have sprouted, thin them according to the packet directions by pulling up and discarding—or gently digging up and relocating—extra seedlings so each surviving plant has room to grow.

JUMP-STARTING WITH TRANSPLANTS

There are situations in which sowing seeds into the garden isn't the best option. For example, you may discover that your growing season isn't quite long enough for warm-season vegetables like tomatoes, peppers, and eggplant to go from seed to maturity. Fortunately, you don't have to forgo these garden favorites. Just give them a jump-start: As soon as the air and soil are warm enough, plant seedlings rather than seeds in your garden. Starting with transplants can shave a few weeks off the time it will take warm-season vegetables to reach maturity in your garden. You can also use this technique with cool-season crops to hurry the first harvest and increase your garden's overall productivity.

Bedding transplants instead of sowing seeds reduces weeding and thinning chores, too. Rather than having to carefully weed around and thin out tiny, delicate sprouts, you can plant seedlings at the proper spacing (as directed on the seed packet or plant label) and surround them with mulch to block weeds.

You have two options for giving garden vegetables a head start: Grow your own seedlings indoors before it is warm enough outside for the plants to thrive, or buy young plants once the air and soil temperatures outside are warm enough for them to be transplanted directly into the garden.

GROWING YOUR OWN TRANSPLANTS

Growing your own seedlings costs less than buying young plants from a nursery or garden center. Tomatoes, hot and sweet peppers, and eggplant are all good candidates for being started from seed indoors and then transplanted outdoors. Start the seeds several weeks before the weather and soil are likely to be warm enough for these plants to thrive outdoors.

To create an indoor nursery in which to grow seedlings, you'll need a few supplies: small pots or shallow seed trays made from plastic, terra cotta, cardboard, or peat that allow water to pass through the bottom; clear lids or coverings to hold in warmth and moisture; plastic or aluminum watering trays (flats); seed-starting mix; and a grow lamp or fluorescent light (once seedlings sprout, they need plenty of bright light each day). In late winter or early spring, you can usually find these items individually or in handy seed-starting kits at garden centers. You can also improvise some supplies. For example, clean plastic food containers with clear lids and holes punched in their bottoms can substitute for store-bought pots or seed trays. And a windowsill or shelf in a south-facing window that receives bright sun all day may work in place of a grow lamp.

Once you've gathered your supplies, place the pots or seed trays on the watering flats, fill the pots or trays with moistened seed-starting mix, sow the seeds at the depth recommended on the seed packet, and cover with the clear lids until the seeds sprout. If you're using a grow light or fluorescent bulb, turn it off at night.

PURCHASING TRANSPLANTS

The other option for giving vegetables a head start skips the seed-sowing stage altogether. You simply purchase young plants and transplant them into your garden. It costs more than starting from seeds, but it does shorten the time until harvest.

You'll probably find a fairly wide sampling of young vegetable plants at your local garden center or nursery—from tomatoes, cabbage crops, and peppers to lettuce, cucumbers, and squash. When choosing seedlings, look for plants that have strong stems, dark green leaves, and healthy root systems. If the plants in general appear wilted, scorched, or otherwise  damaged or diseased or the soil in the pots is bone-dry, the plants may not be receiving adequate care, and you may want to take your business elsewhere.

BEDDING TRANSPLANTS IN THE GARDEN

When the weather is warm enough for your young plants to thrive in the garden, gradually get them used to the conditions outside by "hardening" them before putting them in the ground: Set the pots or trays outdoors in a sheltered spot, out of wind and direct sun, for about an hour, then bring them back inside. Repeat over the next six days before transplanting.

Pick an overcast or drizzly day to transplant your seedlings in the garden; they will recover more quickly. If you must plant on a sunny day, cover the seedlings with cardboard boxes or make cones from newspapers to shield them from the sun for their first day or two in the garden.

Water your seedlings about an hour before transplanting, so the soil is moist but not dripping. Arrange the potted seedlings on the garden bed to get the correct spacing (per the seed packet or plant label). Then dig a hole for each that will allow the seedling to sit at the same depth it did in the container. Just before bedding each plant, carefully upend its pot and tap the bottom so the seedling slides out. Support the root structure and, if necessary, hold the seedling by a leaf (never by its delicate stem) as you place the root ball in the hole. Fill in and firm the soil around the roots, form a shallow ridge of dirt around the plant to hold in water, then give it a deep, gentle watering.

Seedlings started indoors or in crowded greenhouses where they don't get enough light may develop lanky, barren stems that easily topple over. Planting leggy seedlings in slightly deeper holes will give them a stronger foundation outdoors. For leggy tomato seedlings, however, use a horizontal planting trench, not a deeper vertical hole. The soil closer to the surface will be warmer and better aerated than deeper soil, encouraging good root growth. The buried stem will also sprout roots all along its length, resulting in faster plant growth.

If your seedlings were raised in peat pots, tear off the tops and bottoms of the pots before you transplant them. Peat pots are supposed to decay underground, but they don't always break down in the first year after planting. This can leave plant roots captive. And if the pot's rim protrudes above the soil surface, the

pot may dry out and wick moisture from the surrounding soil and nearby roots. Removing the top and bottom of the peat pot before planting will prevent both problems.

Your seedlings will need daily watering for their first several days in the garden, until their roots stretch out into the surrounding soil. Use a soaker hose, or set your hose's nozzle to a gentle spray to prevent washing soil away from the roots.

WATERING AND FEEDING YOUR PLANTS

Besides sunlight and well-prepared soil, plants need water and nutrients to flourish. Since nature isn't always cooperative, you will likely need to supplement rainfall with regular watering. And to promote vigorous growth and productivity, you should feed your plants a well-balanced fertilizer.

WATERING

From the moment their seeds are sown until the end of their growing season, plants need water; without it, they die. But too much water can also be bad for many plants. If they (or even just their roots) are submerged in water for too long, they can rot or drown from lack of oxygen. Meeting your plants' water needs requires moderation. You must give them enough water for good health without flooding them to death.

WHEN TO WATER

The best time to water your garden is in the morning. If you water during the heat of the day, much of the moisture will quickly evaporate. If you water in the cool of the evening, water droplets are likely to stay on leaves, buds, flowers, and fruit throughout the night, encouraging fungal diseases (and slugs) to attack your plants.

Most mature vegetable plants will flourish with one or two good waterings per week. You want to treat them to a generous soaking each time so that the moisture seeps deep into the soil and encourages growth. Giving your garden only a light sprinkling, in contrast, can actually be worse for your plants than missing  a watering session: Because the water doesn't penetrate deeply, a quick sprinkle tends to draw the roots toward the soil surface, where they can be killed by sun exposure.

In general, vegetables need about an inch of water per week—from rainfall and/or watering—to thrive. The idea is to keep the soil lightly moist and prevent it from ever drying out completely.

A good way to determine how much water your plants are receiving from nature is to use a rain gauge. Set the gauge in an open area of your garden, and after each rainfall, check the reading. Keep a log of the amount that has fallen, and supplement nature by watering if the total threatens to fall below one inch per week and/or you notice the soil getting too dry between rainfalls. You can purchase an inexpensive commercial rain gauge at any garden center. Or you can create your own rain gauge by using an uncovered coffee can and a ruler; simply stand the ruler in the can after each rainfall to measure how much rain your garden received.

Of course, nature doesn't always follow human rules, so there are exceptions to the general one-inch-per-week guideline—situations and/or conditions in which an inch of water may be too much or not enough. For example:

- Hot or windy weather and low humidity—both of which hasten evaporation—may make more than an inch of water per week necessary.
- Sandy soil is like a sieve: Water runs right through it. So, if your soil is sandy, you'll likely need to water more often (and possibly exceed the inch-per-week recommendation) to keep it lightly moist. A longer-lasting solution would be to add organic matter to improve the soil's ability to retain moisture.
- Less water is needed when the weather is cool, because the rate of evaporation is much slower. Seeds or roots can rot if they get too much water in cool weather.
- Heavy clay soils retain moisture, so if you've got clay soil, your garden may require less water.
- Container plantings require frequent watering because their soil dries out quickly.

How frequently you need to water depends on the amount of rainfall that your garden receives each week (and its timing, since you want the soil to stay moist throughout the week) but is also affected by how well your soil retains moisture and how fast water evaporates in your climate.

HOW TO WATER

Choosing an appropriate watering method can help ensure your vegetables get the moisture they need while helping you conserve water, effort, and money.

Many people use a sprinkler to water their plants, believing it to be an efficient delivery method. In actuality, it wastes water, because much of its spray evaporates before it ever reaches the plants' roots. And what doesn't evaporate may sit on the foliage, encouraging fungal disease, while the soil below remains dry. Because many sprinklers apply water unevenly (more up close, less farther out), they can also overwater some plants while leaving others thirsty. And how many times have you seen a sprinkler watering not only plants but sidewalks, patios, cars, and even walls? A sprinkler simply isn't a reliable or efficient way to ensure your vegetables get the right amount of water without considerable waste along the way.

If you must use a sprinkler, at least set up multiple rain gauges throughout the garden to be sure all of your plants are getting water. Check the gauges during sprinkling to determine how long it takes the sprinkler to provide a specific amount of water—say, half an inch, for each biweekly watering session—so you can move or turn off the sprinkler to prevent flooding any plants or wasting more water. Having multiple gauges throughout the garden also allows you to compare the amount of moisture each area collects; if readings vary widely, you'll need to move the sprinkler more frequently—or invest in a model that disperses water more evenly.

Better still is to switch to a more efficient and earth-friendly watering method, such as laying down one or more soaker hoses, using an adjustable nozzle on a traditional garden hose, or collecting excess rainwater and/or recycling household water and delivering it to your plants with a watering can. Each of these alternatives allows you to apply water more directly to plant roots, reducing waste.

THE SOAKER HOSE

A soaker hose is made of water-permeable fabric, perforated recycled rubber, or other porous material that allows water to weep out along its length. You lay it across your garden soil and attach it to a regular garden hose that's connected to a spigot set on low or medium. Because it sits right on the soil, the soaker hose delivers water more directly to plant roots. It conserves water (and money) by minimizing evaporation and keeping water from going where it isn't needed. It doesn't spray foliage, so it doesn't encourage fungal infections. And it may even save you some time and labor: Depending on the size and layout of your garden and how many soaker hoses you use, you may be able to lay the soaker(s) down once and leave it in place for the season. With a soaker hose, it can take an hour or more to sufficiently moisten all of the soil near the hose, but once you know how long it takes, you need only be present to turn the spigot on and off.

A soaker hose does require a little special attention to work properly. Here are some tips:

- Lay out your soaker hose(s) as straight as possible. Like most hoses, if it's bent or curved too sharply, it will kink, obstructing the water flow.
- Expect more water to be released from the portion of the hose closest to the spigot and less from the opposite end.
- If the soaker hose only moistens the soil on one side of a plant, even after sufficient watering time, you may need to shift the hose (or use a second hose) to water the dry side.
- To determine if the garden has received enough water, dig into the soil beside the hose, being careful to avoid plant roots. When the water has seeped 12 inches down, turn off the hose. Note how long it took, so you'll know how long to leave the spigot on next time.
- Faster watering can be accomplished with a soaker hose that is flat and peppered with small holes, but its greater water pressure is also more likely to displace the soil around plants.

THE TRADITIONAL HOSE

A traditional garden hose can do the trick if you use a suitable nozzle or spray head and water carefully. Choose a nozzle or spray head designed specifically for garden use, if possible. It must be able to break the heavy flow of water from the hose into fine droplets and spread them evenly across the ground without compacting or greatly disturbing the soil. A spray head with an angled base can make it easier to reach between and beneath plants to direct water toward

roots and away from foliage. If you use hanging planters, consider getting a long-necked spray head that will allow you to water your vegetables without getting on a stepladder.

If you have to drag a traditional garden hose around the yard to water all of your plantings, place hose guides at the edges of your garden beds or at the ends of rows of vegetables to keep the hose from crushing your crops. Hose guides can be as simple as wooden stakes that you pound into the ground at an angle. The portion of each stake above ground should lean away from your plants, so it can stop the hose from sliding into the garden bed. Decorative hose guides made of wood, plastic, or metal are also available.

Another useful accessory to consider if you'll be watering with a traditional garden hose is a hose cart. It can minimize wear and tear on your body from wrestling heavy hose and help prevent frustrating tangles, kinks, and knots in the hose. A hose cart typically includes a crank that neatly retracts the hose and winds it onto a storage reel, which is mounted on a wheeled base and has a long handle for easy pulling. If you'll be rolling the cart over grass or rough ground, get one with large wheels; smaller wheels are fine on sidewalks and patios.

USING RECYCLED WATER

To reduce your use of municipal or well water, you can collect and use rainwater and gray water in your garden. Gray water refers to tap water used in activities like rinsing vegetables and fruits at the kitchen sink and running the tap while the water heats up. Such salvaged water is perfectly safe and just as thirst-quenching for your vegetables, and you can deliver it to your plants' roots quite easily using a watering can. By recycling rainwater and gray water to use in the garden, you'll be helping to conserve a precious natural resource and—if you have to pay for your water—saving yourself money.

Capturing gray water is as easy as keeping a basin nearby that you can pop into the sink during food prep. Avoid collecting water contaminated with water softener salts, strong detergents, fats, oils, or any harsh additives that can harm plants. When your plants need watering or when the basin is nearly full, transfer the water into a watering can, and use it to water new plantings, container vegetables, and any other plants that might need a little extra moisture (such as those fed by the far end of a soaker hose).

You can also put rainwater to use in your garden between rainfalls. Stored rainwater is free of additives such as fluoride and chlorine and is naturally ideal for watering plants. It's at ambient temperature, so it won't shock warmth-loving plants the way cold tap water can. And it's free!

The easiest way to collect rainwater for future use is by placing a large container at the bottom of a downspout. Almost any large, clean bucket will do, but your best bet may be a 30- to 50-gallon barrel or drum, preferably one with mosquito screening covering the top opening and a spigot near the bottom for filling a water can or attaching a hose. (Some municipalities offer sturdy plastic rain barrels to residents at a discount to encourage water conservation.) You can tap every downspout around your house for maximum yield or simply use one or two more discretely located ones.

FERTILIZING

Although you may be able to grow vegetables in your garden without fertilizer, you won't get the best from your plants. Fertilized vegetable plants tend to be healthier and better able to resist disease and attacks from pests, thus producing more and better produce.

There are two types of fertilizer: organic and inorganic. Both contain the same primary nutrients, but their composition and action differ. As long as the necessary nutrients are available, it makes no difference to the plant whether they came from an organic or inorganic source. However, the differences between the two types are worth your consideration.

ORGANIC FERTIZILERS

Organic fertilizers consist of plant and animal materials that contain nutrients. Those materials must be broken down over a period of time by microorganisms in the soil for the nutrients to become available to plants. As a result, organic fertilizers tend to release lower doses of nutrients over an extended period of time, providing a long-term supply that is unlikely to burn plant roots or cause nutrient overdoses the way the concentrated nutrients in chemical fertilizers can. Organic fertilizers, unlike their synthetic counterparts, may also provide a spectrum of lesser nutrients and other natural ingredients that can benefit growing plants. However, because organic fertilizers contain fewer nutrients by weight than do inorganic fertilizers, you'll need to use a larger volume of organic fertilizer to cover the same number of plants.

Manures from herbivores (plant eaters) are the most common organic fertilizer. They are bulkier and contain lower percentages of nutrients than do other natural fertilizers, such as dried blood, kelp, and bone meal. But they have the advantage of immediately improving the texture of the soil.

Fish emulsion fertilizer is an organic option you can use to encourage a burst of growth from recently transplanted vegetables, container plantings, or any plant that seems to be growing sluggishly. High-nitrogen fish emulsion dissolves in water and is easily absorbed and put to immediate use by plants. For best results, follow the package directions. Prepackaged fish emulsion and other organic fertilizers are typically sold at garden centers and nurseries.

You'll probably need to apply a mix of organic fertilizers to ensure balanced nutrition for your vegetables. Use package directions to guide you in creating the right mix for your vegetable plants.

INORGANIC FERTIZILERS

Inorganic, or chemical, fertilizers are concentrated sources of plant nutrients that, when applied to the soil, are immediately available for plants to use. Because inorganic fertilizers are so concentrated, however, it's important to follow the application directions on the package to help prevent burning or overdosing vegetables.

Any container of fertilizer will have three numbers printed on it, such as 5–10–20. These numbers indicate the percentages of the three major nutrients—nitrogen, phosphorus, and potassium—contained in fertilizer. The first number represents the percentage of nitrogen (5, in the above example); the second, the percentage of phosphorus (10); and the third, the percentage of potassium (20). The remaining 65 percent of the fertilizer is typically a mixture of other nutrients and inert filler.

A well-balanced complete fertilizer supplies all three major nutrients in somewhat even proportions, and that's the kind recommended for vegetable gardens, as long as the nitrogen content isn't more than 20 percent. A good bet for your vegetable garden is a fertilizer marked 10-10-10.

HOW TO FERTILIZE

When turning over your garden beds in the spring, apply fertilizer evenly to the entire garden, based on the recommendations provided in your soil-test results. Do not overfertilize. A hand-held spreader makes it easier to neatly and evenly distribute granulated chemical fertilizers over the entire garden bed. To spread heavy organic fertilizer such as manure, use a short-toothed rake. Then, with a spade or tiller, turn the fertilizer into the soil, and smooth out the surface before planting. This first fertilizer application will see most of your vegetables through their initial period of growth.

Roughly midway through the growing season, when many of the nutrients from the original application have been depleted, reapply the fertilizer as a side-dressing. To side-dress, cut a four-inch-deep trench, about 12 to 18 inches from the stem, around each tomato or other large plant or along the side of a row of smaller plants; take care not to disturb plant roots. Spread about half a cup of fertilizer per plant in the trench, refill the trench with the soil, and water thoroughly. Rain and watering will continue to work the fertilizer down into the soil, making it available to plant roots.

For details on how to use specific fertilizers properly, read the package labels before applying (and preferably before purchase). Some fertilizers, such as fish emulsion and water-soluble inorganic products, are designed to be sprayed directly on the plant to feed it through its leaves—something you don't want to discover after you've already side-dressed your entire garden with it. Even if you've used a particular fertilizer in years past or on different plants, read the label again, because the volume required may vary depending on the kind of plant being fertilized and the time of year you're applying it.

CHAPTER 4: MAINTAINING YOUR GARDEN

Much like your home, your garden requires regular housekeeping and maintenance to remain tidy, healthy, and functional. Of course, in the garden, there are no floors to clean or carpets to vacuum, no furniture to polish or roofing to repair, no clothes to be hung up. But there are comparable tasks—such as weeding, mulching, and staking—you should do to keep your garden and its plant inhabitants well-groomed, healthy, and productive.

WEEDING

It's important to keep weeds out of your garden, because they can steal space, sunlight, water, and nutrients from your plants. They can also shelter pests and diseases. Weeds grow and spread quickly, and left unchecked, they can make your garden a very unwelcoming place for the plants you want to grow.

If you diligently attack weeds when they are young, you'll find it relatively easy to keep them under control. If, on the other hand, you let weeds become established, you'll be in for a long, difficult, and frustrating struggle to rid your garden of them. To win the war on weeds, it helps to understand your enemies and know how to keep them on the run.

TYPES OF WEEDS

Like other plants, weeds come in annual and perennial and cool-season and warm-season varieties. Annual weeds spread by seed, which can remain from the previous year or be blown or carried into your garden by birds, animals, or you (on shoes or clothing or hidden in compost or other soil amendments). And, like other annual plants, annual weeds go from germination to death in a single year. (If annual weeds are allowed to go to seed before they are killed or removed, however, the seeds can lie dormant in the soil and, given proper conditions, can germinate the next growing season.) Cool-season annual weeds, such as chickweed, generally germinate in late summer or fall, produce flowers and seeds in spring, and disappear in the heat of summer. Warm-season annuals sprout in spring or early summer, produce flowers and seeds in late summer or early fall, and die in cold temperatures.

In addition to their limited lifespan, most annual weeds have shallow roots. Both characteristics mean that annual weeds are easier to get rid of than are their perennial cousins.

Perennial weeds survive year after year, some by virtue of deep taproots, others through pervasive root networks. They spread by way of those root networks or through seeds and can be incredibly difficult to eradicate. You can dig up the individual plants, but if you leave even the tiniest bit of a perennial weed's

taproot in the soil, it can grow back. Some perennial weeds, such as Canada thistle and dandelion, will spread through the garden like wildfire if they are allowed to go to seed or spread their roots. The key to controlling them, therefore, is to kill them before either can happen. Miss this step, and they can overwhelm your garden—and you.

COMMON GARDEN WEEDS

Annual	Perennials
Carpetweed	Bindweed
Chickweed	Burdock
Common ragweed	Canada thistle
Crabgrass	Dandelion
Giant ragweed	Ground ivy
Lambsquarters	Johnsongrass
Pigweed	Nodding thistle
Purslane	Plantain

TACKLING THE INVADERS

Whether you're fighting annual or perennial weeds, the easiest and most effective approach is to knock them out when they are only tiny seedlings. A push (or Dutch) hoe, slid along just under the soil surface, will pull out young seedlings, particularly annual weed seedlings, roots and all. If you choose a hot, sunny day for hoeing, you won't even have to collect the dug-up seedlings; they'll die from exposure. (If you must hoe seedlings on a cool and/or cloudy day, rake them up so they can't replant.) Use the hoe slowly and with great care as you weed close to your vegetable plants; you don't want to upend them in the process. By running a hoe through your garden at least once a week, you'll nip much of your weed problem in the bud.

A regular garden hoe (the kind with the blade at a 90-degree angle to its handle) may be sufficient for removing older, more established annual weeds. The hoe must be kept sharp, however, because you want to slice mature annual weeds off at the point where their stems meet their roots. And you must cut them down before they go to seed; otherwise, you'll be leaving behind the makings of next year's crop of annual weeds.

Once perennial weeds are past the seedling stage, removing them becomes considerably harder, because they have sturdier, deeper roots and/or networks of connected roots. You can use a garden hoe to chop down deep-rooted perennial weeds every time they establish themselves, and you will probably kill them eventually. But a faster approach is to dig up each weed, being careful to remove the entire taproot. Depending on the weed's size and proximity to your vegetables, you can use a garden fork, the corner of a garden hoe, a shovel or trowel, or a hand-held digging fork (sometimes called a dandelion digger) for this job.

Because mature perennial weeds, especially those with invasive root networks, are so difficult to remove from a planted garden, it is essential to check for them and dig them out—roots and all—during the initial soil-preparation stage.

To help prevent annual and perennial weeds from springing up in your vegetable garden in the first place, enlist the weed-suppressing powers of mulch.

MULCHING

It's hard to overestimate the value of mulching—placing a layer of (preferably organic) material on the soil around your vegetable plants. By holding in moisture, mulch can reduce the amount of water you need to supply to your garden by as much as 50 percent. Even a thin layer of mulch will help to limit evaporation from the soil surface.

Organic mulch, specifically, acts as both shield and nourishment for garden soil, helping to ensure the health and productivity of your growing vegetables.

BENEFITS OF ORGANIC MULCH

Organic mulch performs a number of valuable functions in the vegetable garden:

- It slows evaporation—helping to keep the soil evenly moist for fast, steady plant growth—and helps conserve water.
- It discourages weed germination.
- It insulates the soil, keeping it warmer during cool weather and cooler during warm weather.
- It adds organic matter to the soil, immediately improving soil texture, and, as it decomposes, it gradually releases nutrients into the soil, helping to feed growing plants.
- It helps protect against soil erosion by dissipating the force of hard, heavy rains.
- It provides a layer of cushion that helps to prevent soil compaction.
- It helps to reduce certain plant-disease problems.

ORGANIC MULCH MATERIALS

The following are organic materials commonly used as mulches in vegetable gardens:

Grass clippings. Don't use clippings from a lawn treated with weed killer, which can kill your vegetables. Let untreated clippings dry before spreading them around your garden; fresh grass gets matted down and smells bad when decomposing.

Straw. Straw is excellent mulch, although it can be a bit messy and hard to apply in small areas. As it decomposes, it can also lower the nitrogen level in the soil, meaning you may need to supplement with nitrogen. Be sure to use straw and not hay, which contains many weed seeds.

Compost. Though it can look a little rough, partially decomposed compost makes a great mulch and soil conditioner.

Chopped leaves. Fall leaves make a good end-of-season mulch for the garden, helping to block the growth of winter weeds and keeping the soil light and fluffy. Since whole leaves can be blown out of place, you'll have better luck if you run them through a lawn mower and, if possible, allow them to partially decompose before applying them as mulch. Do not use walnut leaves; they are toxic to some vegetable plants.

Sawdust. Sawdust may be readily available in some areas, but it acidifies the ground as it decomposes and steals nitrogen from the soil. If laboratory analysis indicates your soil would benefit from such effects, sawdust may be the perfect mulch for your garden (you still may need to replace nitrogen, however). If possible, allow sawdust to decompose for a year before using it as mulch in your garden.

SPREADING MULCH

Wait until the soil has warmed up in spring to apply organic mulch. If you put it down too soon, it will prevent the soil from warming, which will slow the development of your plants' roots. Spread a two- to three-inch-thick layer of mulch on the surface of the soil surrounding your plants and on any bare areas of soil to keep them free of weeds.

Be careful not to smother the vegetables and herbs in your efforts to squelch weeds. Wait until vegetable seeds have sprouted and seedlings are three or four  inches tall before mulching around them. Spread the mulch around the plants, but keep it an inch or two away from each plant's main stem or crown. As the mulch flattens and breaks down, apply more mulch. (In warm, humid climates, this may be necessary every few weeks.) Aim to keep a two-inch layer in place through the rest of the season.

SUPPORTING YOUR PLANTS

Vining plants, such as peas, pole beans, cucumbers, melons, pumpkins, and many kinds of squash, will take up a large amount of garden space if you let them trail along the ground. Tomato plants, too, will stretch out in all directions if left to their own devices. To keep these wanderers tidy, restrain them from taking up excess space, prevent their fruit from rotting or being attacked by insects and slugs on the ground, and provide them with sturdy support. Such support can come from store-bought or homemade trellises, poles, stakes, cages, or even nearby fencing. Sink the supports into the soil soon after seeds have sprouted or when you transplant seedlings in the ground to minimize the risk of hitting and damaging plant roots in the process.

You can buy trellises to support and corral vining plants or make your own using plastic netting or string, wire or heavy twine, and wooden stakes or posts. Simply drive wooden stakes into the soil along a row of pole beans or peas, and staple the netting to the supports. Or drive two thick, sturdy wooden posts into the ground at either end of a row or patch of vining plants; connect them top and bottom with wire or heavy twine; then lace string up and down. If the vines don't begin climbing the trellis on their own, train them to do so by loosely tying them to the trellis using lengths of pantyhose, soft cloth, twine, or twist ties (like those used to close plastic bags).

The twiggy sticks you get from pruning your hedges or shrubs make excellent supports for a row of garden peas. This is an old British trick called pea staking. Simply poke the sticks into the soil along the row of young pea plants, and the vines will soon climb them.

Three or four bamboo poles or long plastic plant stakes arranged in a teepee shape make a good support for pole-beans vines, which will twine around the stakes as they climb upward. Just fasten the stakes together near the top with twine, spread out the legs, and poke them into the soil so that the teepee is stable. Then plant your beans around it.

For supporting tomato plants, tomato cages are deservedly popular. You simply set each cage in place over a young tomato plant and push the legs into the soil. The cage will provide support for branches heavy with juicy tomatoes, keep the main stem(s) from toppling over, and prevent the plant from spreading too far.

A single, sturdy stake can also provide suitable support for a tomato plant. Use a two-inch by two-inch wooden or plastic-coated metal stake, eight feet in length, and drive it 24 to 30 inches into the soil. As the plant grows, attach it loosely to the stake with strips of pantyhose or soft cloth.

Extra-large tomato cages can also be used to support heavier plants that grow on vines, such as squash, melons, and cucumbers. Simply set a cage around each group of seedlings (or around each hill of seeds), push the wire points into the soil, and let the vines cover the cage.

DISEASES

One of the most challenging—and sometimes frustrating—aspects of being a gardener is battling the plant diseases and pests that want your crops as much as you do. But you're not defenseless. To assist you in the fight, you can take advantage of the wisdom developed by generations of gardeners. Putting that wisdom to work can help you protect your vegetables from nature's voracious invaders.

Like people, plants are subject to diseases, some of which can threaten their productivity or even their lives. Once a disease hits a plant, it can be difficult to cure, although you can take steps to save the rest of the crop. But the better solution is to prevent the disease in the first place.

DISCOURAGING DISEASE

In the garden, an ounce of prevention can be worth pounds of vegetables and herbs. Fortunately, there are a variety of defenses you can employ to protect your plants from the most common vegetable-plant diseases.

The easiest way to avoid disease problems is to choose, whenever possible, varieties of vegetables and herbs that are resistant to disease. Over the years, many disease-resistant vegetable cultivars (cultivated varieties) have been developed. Planting these instead of relying on chemical dusts and sprays to stop disease means you don't have to worry about potentially poisoning children, pets, yourself, or the planet.

There are varying levels of protection available:

- Some cultivators are resistant to multiple diseases, providing maximum protection. The "Big Beef" tomato, for instance, resists various types of wilts, tobacco mosaic virus, nematodes, and gray leaf spot. There is little left to harm this variety in terms of disease.
- Some cultivators resist only one disease. But if the disease is prevalent in your area, that resistance can save your crop.
- Other plants are disease tolerant, rather than disease resistant, meaning they may still get the disease but should grow well despite it.

Seed packets, plant labels, and catalog descriptions for some vegetable cultivars include one or more of the letters V, F, N, and T as part of the variety's name. These letters indicate disease resistance that has been bred into that particular cultivar:

- **V** and **F** stand for resistance to verticillium and fusarium wilts, which are fungi that infect tomato plants and cause them to turn yellow, wilt, and die.
- **N** indicates nematode tolerance. Nematodes are tiny parasitic worms that cause knots on vegetable-plant stems and roots.
- **T** is for resistance to tobacco mosaic virus, which causes yellowing and curling of foliage and severe root damage.

Favoring cultivators that are resistant to multiple diseases—and therefore have multiple letters in their name—will increase your chances of growing healthy, productive vegetable plants.

SOME DISEASE-RESISTANT CULTIVATORS

- Cucumbers: 'Streamliner Hybrid'; 'Sweeter Yet' Hybrid; 'Fancipack'; 'Homemade Pickles'; 'Tasty King'; 'Sweet Success'; 'Salad Bush'
- Peas: 'Super Sugar Snap'; 'Sugar Pop'; 'Maestro'; 'Green Arrow'; 'Oregon Sugar Pod II'
- Beans: 'Buttercrisp'; 'Jade', 'Florence'; 'Blue Lake 274'
- Tomatoes: Celebrity'; 'Better Boy'; 'LaRossa'; 'Sunmaster'; 'Enchantment'; 'Mountain Delight'; 'Beefmaster'; 'Big Beef '; 'Sweet Million'; 'Viva Italia'; 'Roma'; 'Lemon Boy'
- Strawberries: 'Surecrop'; 'Cavendish'; 'Redchief '; 'Allstar'; 'Guardian'; 'Scott'; 'Lateglow'; 'Delite'

ROTATE YOUR CROPS

It may make garden planning easier, but planting the same crop in the same spot each year gives diseases a chance to build up strength. Pest insects may also overwinter in the soil or debris beneath the plants they infested during the growing season, leaving them perfectly perched to cause trouble the following year if you put the same type of plant in that spot again. Do not grow members of the same plant family in the same spot in your garden year after year.

The three major vegetable families are:

- Cole crops (cabbage family): broccoli, brussels sprouts, cabbage, cauliflower, kohlrabi, rutabaga, and turnip
- Cucurbits (cucumber family): cucumber, gourd, muskmelon, pumpkin, summer and winter squash, and watermelon
- Solanaceous plants (tomato and pepper family): eggplant, pepper, potato, and tomato

After growing a crop from one of these families one year, choose a vegetable from a different family to plant in the same spot the following season. Plan your garden so each family of vegetables can be moved to another block of your garden on a three-year rotation.

AVOID OVERCROWDING

In an overcrowded garden, airflow is impeded and the air becomes stagnant, just as it does in an overcrowded room. Without good air circulation, foliage that's damp from dew, rain, or watering will stay wet longer and be more susceptible to fungus and other diseases. Overcrowding can also prevent each plant from getting all the sunlight, water, and nutrients it needs, leaving it weaker and more susceptible to diseases and pests.

Be sure that when you seed and/or transplant vegetables in the garden, you follow the spacing directions from the seed packet, plant label, or seed catalog. If vining plants or bushier plants like tomatoes begin to overtake their neighbors, install trellising, stakes, or cages to corral them and direct their growth upward.

53

CONTROLLING DISEASE

If plants seem stunted and weak or their leaves turn yellow or grayish or have a white powdery coating, they may have a disease. If you're not sure what is causing a plant to appear sickly, bring a sample to your local nursery or local cooperative extension service; the staff should be able to help you identify the culprit.

Plant diseases are typically a bit more difficult to control than are attacks by insects. But there are usually ways to disrupt outbreaks so you don't lose an entire crop. The following are some of the most common vegetable-plant diseases and what to do if you discover them in your garden:

Mildew. Mildew causes leaves to turn grayish or appear coated in whitish powder. To treat affected plants and halt an outbreak, mix two teaspoons baking soda and half teaspoon corn oil in two quarts water. Put in a sprayer, shake well, and apply to both affected and susceptible plants often; always reapply after a rain, as well. Remove and discard any severely damaged leaves.

Viruses. Stunted or yellowing plants are likely to be suffering from a virus. Viruses can affect any plant in your garden. There is no cure. Remove the infected plants and dispose of them in the trash, not in the compost pile, to prevent the problem from spreading. Viruses can spread from cigarettes and other tobacco products, too, so do not smoke in the garden or handle plants after smoking without washing your hands first.

Nutrient imbalances. If your tomatoes, peppers, or squash develop dark, sunken patches at the blossom end of their fruit, they're probably suffering from a nutrient imbalance. Dig some compost into the soil around the plant to balance out nutrients for the current growing season. After the growing season, have your soil tested to determine exactly which nutrient(s) is lacking or overabundant, and before planting the following year, add amendments to the soil as directed by the laboratory to bring nutrients into proper balance.

Blight. Wet-looking spots on the leaves of tomatoes, eggplant, peppers, beans, or squash are a symptom of blight. There is no cure, and the problem can quickly worsen or spread. Remove and dispose of affected leaves at once. In the future, choose resistant or tolerant varieties, and rotate crops to keep blight away.

PESTS

Insects are naturally drawn to garden plants, and that's not always a problem, because some of them play a beneficial role in the garden. But other insects—as well as slugs and four-legged pests—spell nothing but trouble for your vegetables. They should be discouraged from visiting your garden and made unwel-

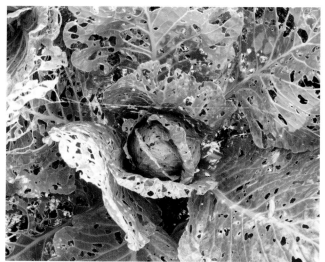

come if they do show up. Be sure to monitor your plants for signs of pests, and take simple steps to reduce or eliminate invaders with nonchemical measures.

KEEPING PEST INSECTS AWAY

Start your battle against the tiny troublemakers by making your garden less accessible and attractive to them and more attractive to the predator insects that feed on them.

Use floating row covers. This simple idea works so well it's a wonder nobody thought of it years ago. Floating row covers are lightweight fabrics that you drape over plants to keep out pests. They allow sun, rain, and fresh air to penetrate, but if secured to the ground with rocks, bricks, or long metal staples, they keep flying insects out.

For example, row covers can keep egg-laying female flies, and the maggots they produce, away from your vegetables. That's great news for your garden, because maggots tunnel into and damage the roots of radishes, turnips, carrots, onions, and other vegetables. If you pin the edges of row covers down tightly, you'll also keep potato beetles from flying or crawling into the garden to eat the foliage off potato plants.

Bring in beneficials. Interspersing flowering plants among your vegetables will help attract ladybugs, spiders, lacewings, tiny parasitic wasps, and other tiny creatures that prey on plant-eating insects. The flowers provide shelter, nectar, and pollen to these beneficials.

Once beneficial insects are at home in your garden, keep them there. Remember, they can be killed as quickly by broad-spectrum pesticides as their prey can be. It's best, therefore, to avoid pesticides. If you must resort to them, use only targeted ones that spare beneficials.

CONTROLLING PEST INSECTS AND SLUGS

If you notice signs of insect or slug infestation, such as holes in leaves, chewed leaf edges, trails of slime, or the little creatures themselves, act. If the pests are visible (use a flashlight to check the leaves and soil surface for slugs at night, when they're active) and large enough to grab, pick them off by hand, and drop them into a container of soapy (for insects) or very salty (for slugs) water. The following tips can help you deal with other little vegetable-garden pests:

Cutworms. Feeding at night and hiding during the day, cutworms are most destructive early in the season, cutting off transplants at ground level. To prevent cutworms from devouring your young cabbage, pepper, and tomato plants, wrap each stem with a paper or thin-cardboard collar as you transplant it (or right after it sprouts). The collar should reach at least one inch below and one inch above the soil's surface. In time, the collar will disintegrate; by then, the danger of cutworm damage will have passed.

Nematodes. These microscopic wormlike pests, which can damage tomatoes, potatoes, and other crops, are killed by chemicals released by marigold roots and decaying foliage. To keep nematodes in check, plant French or American marigolds in and around your nematode-susceptible plants. Or just till marigolds into the soil and let them decay (you can also do this before planting potatoes or tomatoes).

Slugs. Slugs are not insects, but as voracious little plant eaters, they are most definitely garden pests. Slugs will eat almost anything, munching on tender succulent plants and eating them down to the ground. They thrive where the soil is damp, spending sunny days under rocks, logs, or mulch and coming out to eat when it's rainy or cool and dark. Your slug control measures will work better if you rid your garden of dark, damp slug hiding (and breeding) places, such as boards laid on your garden paths or between your plants.

To kill existing slugs, drown them in beer. (Slugs apparently love beer!) Bury an empty plastic margarine tub in the garden soil so that the top rim is level with the soil surface. Fill the tub with beer (any kind will do), and leave it overnight. The slugs should crawl in and drown. Empty the tub every day or two, and refill it with beer until it comes up empty in the morning.

Another option is to try diatomaceous earth—a gritty substance that pierces the skin of soft-bodied slugs—to keep slugs from returning to your plants to feed. Sprinkle it on the soil, encircling affected and susceptible plants. Use horticultural-grade diatomaceous earth, not the kind sold with swimming-pool supplies.

Copper strips, set around the edge of the garden, may also help discourage further slug activity by giving their mucus-covered bodies a shock as they attempt to slide over. The copper strips should be wide enough to sit one inch deep in the soil and extend several inches above it, preventing slugs from bypassing it.

DEFENDING AGAINST FOUR-LEGGED PESTS

A good fence is a necessary defense against rabbits, groundhogs, deer, and other four-legged critters attracted to your vegetable garden. But a fence isn't foolproof. Animals may climb it, burrow under it, or even leap it in a single bound. So, you'll need additional ammunition.

To increase your defenses, spray organic repellents on your garden plants to discourage deer and other animals from eating them. Sprays made from hot peppers, coyote or bobcat urine, rotten eggs, bonemeal, blood meal—even castor oil—can make your garden unappetizing to herbivores. Reapply them frequently, and always after it rains, to maintain high protection levels.

Strong-smelling soaps can help deter deer, too. Put powerfully scented soaps in mesh bags that you dangle from three-foot-high stakes placed in and around your garden and from any low shrubs nearby. You can also set soap bars directly on the ground. The soap will eventually dissolve or lose its smell, so check it from time to time and replenish it as needed.

Instead of putting soap in the mesh bags, you can try substituting human hair, which some gardeners swear by as a deer deterrent. Just pull a handful from a hairbrush, or ask a local salon for longish clippings. The scent, it's thought, tricks the deer into believing you're in the garden, prompting them to flee. Refill the bags as needed to keep deer away.

CHAPTER 5: HARVESTING YOUR GARDEN

Picking your first ripe tomato, digging up your first crunchy carrots, stepping outside to gather fresh greens for a dinner salad—there's nothing like the thrill of harvesting food you've grown yourself. And, if picked with care, there's nothing like the flavor of a vegetable or herb at its peak.

The final fall harvest does not mean your time in the garden is over for the year, however. Once you've gathered those last few vegetables and herbs, you'll need to prepare your garden for winter. It may be tempting to put off or even skip these chores, but taking care of them at the end of the growing season can make a big difference in the success of the following year's garden.

HARVESTING

Vegetables mature at different times, and if you plant an assortment of them, you'll probably be happily harvesting throughout much of the growing season. You might get your first batch of radishes in early spring and not pull in your last pumpkin until the first fall frost threatens.

How do you know when a vegetable is ripe for picking? With some crops, such as tomatoes, cucumbers, or pumpkins, it's easy: You can tell just by looking at them. But for other crops, such as red beets and sweet corn, the signs of readiness aren't quite as obvious.

You'll find advice on gauging the ripeness of different vegetables and herbs in the final chapters of this book. Even with this information, you may find it a little tricky at first to decide when a vegetable is ready. But as you continue harvesting, you'll get better at it. And by the end of your first gardening season, you'll be confidently picking your produce at the peak of ripeness.

HANDLE WITH CARE

As you harvest, be careful to avoid damaging the vegetables or the plants themselves. Handle the vegetables gently to prevent bruising of the skin or flesh. Use caution, too, when you are picking ripe vegetables from a plant; you don't want to tear or snap any branches in the process.

As you enjoy harvesting and eating the fruits of your labors, you'll quickly learn which crops to plant more or less of. Make notes about your results in your garden journal, and refer to them when you plan next year's vegetable patch.

STORE PROPERLY

Vegetable plants produce a surprisingly abundant harvest. To make sure none goes to waste, you'll need to know how to properly store the extras to preserve their goodness. Some vegetables, such as salad greens, can be stored in the refrigerator but will last only a few days; others, including butternut squash and potatoes, can stay in storage for months.

Different vegetables require different storage conditions. Refrigeration is a preservation measure that works in the short term for many vegetables. But long-term storage often requires other options. Typically, the temperature and humidity of the storage area determine whether a crop will keep there, especially for extended periods. One of these general conditions will suit nearly all vegetables:

- Cold and moist (32°–40°F and 95 percent relative humidity)
- Cold and dry (32°–40°F and 65 percent relative humidity)
- Cool and dry (50°–60°F and 60 percent relative humidity)

Most popular garden vegetables do best in cold, moist conditions. They usually have a short storage life, from several days to about two weeks. While a refrigerator is cold enough, it's usually too dry for them. To compensate, you can place these vegetables in perforated plastic bags (which create a more humid environment) before storing them in the fridge.

Root crops such as beets and carrots also require moist cold and can actually last a long time when stored in such conditions. If you run out of room in the refrigerator for these vegetables, store them in a damp, unheated cellar or garage. Layer them in boxes of straw, which will provide ventilation and insulation from extreme cold.

For vegetables that prefer cold, dry air, the refrigerator truly does provide ideal long-term storage conditions.

For crops that need cool and dry conditions for long-term storage, a basement will usually do. (You'll find some additional storage tips in the vegetable and herb profiles at the end of this book.) You might also consider canning, drying, freezing, or pickling the extra vegetables from your garden.

WHERE TO STORE WHAT

Cold and moist
Store these in the refrigerator in plastic bags to retain humidity, but poke some holes in the bags for ventilation to inhibit mold growth:

- Asparagus
- Beans, snap
- Beets
- Broccoli
- Brussels sprouts
- Cabbage
- Carrots
- Cauliflower
- Corn
- Cucumbers
- Eggplant
- Kohlrabi
- Lettuce
- Melons
- Peas
- Potatoes
- Radishes
- Spinach
- Strawberries
- Summer squash
- Tomatoes
- Zucchini

Cold and dry
Store these unbagged (or in mesh bags) in your refrigerator or in another cold, dry place, where they will last a long time:
- Garlic
- Onions

Cool and dry
Store these in a dry basement or other cool, dry space:
- Pumpkins
- Winter squash

FALL CLEANUP

The better job you do of cleaning up your garden in the fall, the easier it will be to get it up and growing the following spring. Besides, spring comes with its own list of garden tasks, and postponing cleanup will only add to it. So, follow these guidelines to put your garden to bed for the winter:

- Remove plants that have finished their useful lives. Pull out tomato plants, lettuce, and any other crops past their prime, and add them to your compost pile (see the following chapter on composting for more details).
- Remove any weeds. If annual weeds haven't yet set seed, toss them on the compost heap; otherwise, discard them. Do not put the roots of perennial weeds in the compost pile, unless you want to spread weeds with the compost.
- After the first fall frost, use the directions in the section that begins below to prepare perennial plants for winter.
- Take steps to protect the bare garden from weeds and to ready the soil for next year's planting.

PROTECT AND PREPARE YOUR SOIL

Once you've cleared your garden of plants in the fall, it's a good idea to turn over the soil. If you put off this task until early the next spring, and the soil ends up being too wet to be worked, you may have to delay both your soil preparation and your planting, thus shortening the length of your growing season.

Once the soil freezes in fall, apply a layer of mulch over the bare garden (do this whether you turned the soil over or not). Use a light, fluffy mulch, such as straw, chopped leaves, or compost. Mulch will prevent most weed seeds from germinating in the garden during fall and winter, saving you time and work come spring. Rake off this mulch in early spring to allow the soil to warm up.

An alternative to spreading mulch is to plant a fast-growing cover crop to blanket the soil and prevent cool-season weeds from germinating during fall and winter. Good options include buckwheat, crimson clover, rye, and winter wheat. The cover crop is one you don't intend to harvest; you're simply growing it as a protective coat for the soil.

You needn't plant the cover crop all at once; you can seed each area of the garden as the space becomes available. Just till or spade the soil in a cleared area, then scatter your cover-crop seeds over it. Gently rake the surface to work the seeds into the top inch of soil, add a light covering of straw to help hold in moisture and speed germination, and water the area well to settle the soil. When spring planting time arrives, simply turn the cover crop into the soil with a spade or rototiller. The plants will decompose in the soil, enriching it with organic matter.

CHAPTER 6: COMPOSTING FOR YOUR GARDEN

When ordinary garden soil is enriched with generous amounts of organic matter, it becomes moist, fertile, and airy—the ideal medium for growing healthy, productive vegetable plants. Soil fortified in this way also nurtures a rich population of beneficial organisms, such as aerating earthworms, nutrient-releasing bacteria, and root-extending fungi.

Organic matter is so important because it contains the nutrients that growing plants need. But organic matter must decompose—be broken down by microorganisms that act as nature's recyclers—in order for its nutrients to be released back into the soil to feed plants. Decomposition is a natural process that can take years.

Fortunately, gardeners have a way to hurry the decomposition process and get those valuable nutrients back into the soil sooner. It's an easy, economical, and earth-friendly practice called composting. In less than a year, composting can turn leftover organic matter like yard waste and  kitchen scraps into nutrient-rich compost that can then be added to garden soil to nourish plants. In addition to serving up essential nutrients to hungry plants, compost can perform other jobs in the garden.

- Incorporating compost improves soil's ability to control moisture. Adding compost to sandy soil increases its ability to hold water. Mixing compost into clay-heavy soil improves drainage. The more compost you dig in, the more you improve the soil's texture.
- Compost has natural antibacterial properties that help keep your garden free of disease.
- Used as mulch, compost helps conserve water, inhibit weeds, and protect plant roots from hot, dry summer conditions.
- Compost stimulates seed germination when added to the potting soil used to start seeds indoors.

WHAT TO COMPOST

A surprising variety of life's organic leftovers can be used to make compost. Yard waste—except weeds gone to seed, roots of perennial plants (including perennial weeds), and anything treated with herbicide—is fair game. Kitchen waste works, too, although you'll want to steer clear of greasy or meaty scraps that will attract animal pests.

Organic material will decay fastest if you use approximately two parts of fresh "green" material, which contributes nitrogen, to roughly one part of dry "brown" material, which adds carbon. The following are good sources to add to your compost pile:

Green Material

- Manure from chickens, cows, horses, rabbits, pigs, guinea pigs, and other herbivores (no dog or cat waste)
- Uncooked fruit and vegetable scraps and peels; eggshells
- Grass clippings
- Annual weeds not gone to seed
- Perennial weed tops (no roots)
- Plant clippings
- Green leaves
- Strips of turf (check for perennial weeds first)
- Alfalfa

Brown Material

- Autumn leaves (chopped)
- Straw
- Soft (not woody) pruning scraps
- Wood chips
- Ground-up twigs
- Sawdust

HOW TO COMPOST

For the most part, nature's recyclers will take organic matter, no matter how it is presented, and turn it into rich, dark compost. You can simply make a pile of composting materials in some out-of-the-way corner of the yard, and leave it be. But with that approach, you'll have a longer wait for compost.

The better approach is to create conditions that encourage speedy work by the microorganisms responsible for decomposition. Those conditions include moisture, warmth, and air circulation.

Decomposition will occur more quickly if you keep the pile moist (like a squeezed-out sponge) but not soaking wet. So, as you add material to your compost pile, and especially after you add a generous layer of dry (brown) materials, water the pile with a spray from your garden hose.

Heat also tends to speed up the decomposition process. An ideal compost pile should be three to four feet high (and roughly as wide and deep). That size, while still manageable, is large enough to get warm from the heat of the decay process (the pile should steam on a cool morning). High temperatures also semi-sterilize the compost, killing disease spores, hibernating pests, and weed seeds.

For decomposers to work efficiently enough to create heat, they also need plenty of air—and not just at the surface of the pile. Aeration is traditionally provided by fluffing or turning the pile with a pitchfork, which can be hard work. You can make it easier with a little advance planning and a perforated pipe.

First, start your compost pile on a bed of branched sticks, which will allow air to rise from below. Second, stand a perforated PVC pipe in the center of the pile, and build layers of compost material around it. The air will flow through the pipe to aerate the core of the pile.

It's up to you whether you enclose your compost pile in a bin of some sort or leave it open on all sides. A bin will help to contain (and hide) the layers of decaying compost material and may help keep some curious paws and noses out of the pile.

Many styles of compost bins are available for purchase, including models that can be rotated to aerate the mixture. You can also make your own bin from wire fencing, wooden pallets,

lumber, or concrete blocks. It should be slightly larger than the compost pile you're planning to create. A bin that includes an access door at the bottom will allow you to scoop out the lower layers of finished compost while the upper layers are still decaying.

JUMP-STARTING YOUR COMPOST

To help jump-start the decay of organic materials, consider adding compost starter or good garden soil to your new compost pile.

Compost starter, available from garden centers and catalogues, contains decay-causing microorganisms. Some brands also contain nutrients, enzymes, hormones, and other stimulants that help decomposers work as fast as possible. Special formulations can be particularly helpful for hard-to-compost, woody material like wood chips and sawdust or for quick decay of brown leaves.

ON-THE-SPOT COMPOSTING

Use on-site composting for easy soil improvement. Pile dead leaves, livestock manure, and/or green vegetable scraps in or beside the garden until they rot, then work them into the soil. Or, in the fall, just heap them on the garden bed and till them into the soil; they'll decay by spring. You can also dig a hole, dump in yard waste, cover it with a little soil, and let it rot in private.

Good garden soil is not as high-tech or expensive as compost starter, but it contains native decomposers that are quite able to jump-start a compost pile. Just sprinkle the soil among the yard scraps as you build the pile.

CHAPTER 7: VEGETABLE PROFILES

Name: Artichoke

Botanical Name: *Cynara scolymus*

Description: The artichoke is a thistlelike, tender perennial that grows three to four feet tall and three to four feet wide. It is grown for its flower buds, which are eaten before they begin to open. The elegant, architectural leaves make the artichoke very decorative, but because it is tender and hates cold weather, it's not for all gardens.

How to Plant: Artichokes are grown from offshoots, suckers, or seed. For best results, start with offshoots or suckers from a reputable nursery or garden center; artichoke plants grown from seed vary tremendously in quality. Artichokes need rich, well-drained soil that will hold moisture, and a position in full sunlight. Space the offshoots or suckers three to four feet apart in rows four to five feet apart.

Serving Suggestions: Cook artichokes in salted water with a squeeze of lemon juice to help retain their color. With hot artichokes serve a Hollandaise sauce; a vinaigrette is delicious when they're cold. They're not as messy to eat as you may imagine—anyway, it's quite legitimate to use your fingers. Stuff artichokes with seafood or a meat mixture and bake them. To stuff, spread open the leaves and remove some of the center leaves; cut off some of the hard tips of the outer leaves. Baby artichokes are delicious in stews, or marinated in olive oil, vinegar, and garlic as part of an antipasto.

Name: Asparagus

Botanical Name: *Asparagus officinalis*

Description: Asparagus is a long-lived hardy perennial with fleshy roots and fern-like, feathery foliage. The plant grows about three feet tall, and the part you eat is the tender young stem.

How to Plant: Asparagus needs well-drained soil, with a pH over 6. Full sun is best, but asparagus will tolerate a little shade. Asparagus is usually grown from crowns; look for well-grown, well-rooted specimens, and be sure they don't dry out. To plant asparagus crowns, dig out a trench or furrow 10 inches wide and 10 to 12 inches deep, and put in two to four inches of loose soil. Space the crowns in the prepared bed in rows 18 inches apart, leaving 12 to 18 inches between plants. Place the crowns on the soil, with the roots well spread out, and cover with two more inches of soil.

Serving Suggestions: One of the earliest records of asparagus being eaten in America recommends it with "oyl and vinegar," which is still one of the best ways. Steam asparagus quickly, or cook it upright in a pan, so the stems cook faster than the tender tips. Fresh asparagus adorned with nothing but a little melted butter is superb—or try it with creamed chicken on toast or laid on toast and topped with a thin slice of prosciutto and cream sauce.

Name: <u>Dry Beans</u>

Botanical Name: *Phaseolus species*

Description: Dry beans are tender annuals. Their leaves are usually composed of three leaflets, and the small flowers are pale yellow or white. Dry beans are seldom planted in the home vegetable garden because it's so easy and inexpensive to buy them. They're fairly easy to grow, however, and give good yields, so if you have space in your garden you may want to try them.

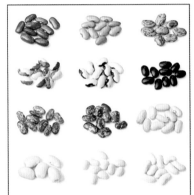

You can grow either bush or pole varieties of beans. Bushes are generally easier to handle; they grow only one to two feet tall, and they mature earlier. Pole beans require a trellis for support; they grow more slowly, but produce more beans per plant.

How to Plant: After the last frost is over, choose a bed in full sunlight; beans tolerate partial shade, but partial shade tends to mean a partial yield. Bean seeds may crack and germinate poorly when the moisture content of the soil is too high. Don't soak the seeds before planting, and don't overwater immediately afterwards.

Plant the bean seeds an inch deep. If they're bush beans, plant the seeds three to four inches apart in rows at least 18 to 24 inches apart. Seeds of pole beans should be planted four to six inches apart in rows 30 to 36 inches apart. When the seedlings are large enough to handle, thin the plants to four to six inches apart. Cut the seedlings with scissors at ground level; be careful not to disturb the others. Beans don't mind being a little crowded—in fact, they'll use each other for support.

Serving Suggestions: Dried beans are tremendously versatile and have the added advantage of being interchangeable in many recipes. They're also nourishing and figure prominently in vegetarian recipes. Chili and baked beans are two of the famous dishes that depend upon dried beans, and beans are essential to the famous French cassoulet—a hearty stew that combines beans with pork, chicken, sausage, or a mixture of all three depending on the region the cook comes from. Try refried pinto beans as a filling for tacos. Add sausage or ham to a thick bean soup for a winter supper to cheer up the chilliest evening.

74

Name: <u>Green and Snap Beans</u>

Botanical Name: *Phaseolus vulgaris*

Description: Green beans are tender annuals that grow either as bushes or vines. Snap beans require a short growing season—about 60 days of moderate temperatures from seed to the first crop. They'll grow anywhere in the United States and are an encouraging vegetable for the inexperienced gardener. The immature pod is the part that's eaten. Beans grow as bushes or vines.

How to Plant: After the last frost is over, choose a bed in full sunlight; beans tolerate partial shade, but partial shade tends to mean a partial yield.

Plant seeds of all varieties an inch deep. If you're planting bush beans, plant the seeds two inches apart in rows at least 18 to 24 inches apart. Seeds of pole beans should be planted four to six inches apart in rows 30 to 36 inches apart. Or plant them in inverted hills, five or six seeds to a hill, with 30 inches of space around each hill. For pole varieties, set the supports or trellises at the time of planting.

Serving Suggestions: Really fresh, tender snap beans are delicious eaten raw; they make an unusual addition to a platter of crudités for dipping. They're also good lightly cooked and tossed with diced potatoes and a little onion and bacon for a delightful hot bean salad. You can also cut snap beans in lengths and sauté them all together with diced potatoes, carrots, and onions for an interesting vegetable dish. On their own, snap beans take well to many spices, including basil, dill, marjoram, and mint.

Name: <u>Lima Beans</u>

Botanical Name: *Phaseolus lunatus*

Description: This tender, large-seeded annual bean grows as either a bush or a vine. With this type of bean the mature seed is eaten, not the entire pod. Lima beans need warmer soil than snap beans in order to germinate properly, and they need higher temperatures and a longer growing season for a good crop.

Bush lima beans are generally easier to handle than pole varieties; bushes grow only one to two feet tall, and they mature earlier. Pole beans require a trellis for support; they grow more slowly, but produce more beans per plant.

How to Plant: After the last frost is over, choose a bed in full sunlight; beans tolerate partial shade, but partial shade tends to mean a partial yield.

Plant seeds of all varieties an inch deep. If you're planting bush limas, plant the seeds two inches apart in rows at least 18 to 24 inches apart. Seeds of pole beans should be planted four to six inches apart in rows 30 to 36 inches apart, or plant them in inverted hills, five or six seeds to a hill, with 30 inches of space around each hill.

When the seedlings are growing well, thin the plants to four to six inches apart. Cut the seedlings with scissors at ground level; be careful not to disturb the others. Beans don't mind being a little crowded; in fact, they'll use each other for support.

Serving Suggestions: Try limas raw for an unusual treat. Serve them in a salad with thinly sliced red onion, parsley, and a vinaigrette dressing, or marinate them for 24 hours in oil, lemon juice, and freshly chopped dill. Cook limas just until tender and serve with a creamy sauce. For a tangy treatment, bake them in a casserole with honey, mustard, and yogurt.

Name: <u>Beets</u>

Botanical Name: *Beta vulgaris*

Description: The beet is grown as an annual, although technically it's a biennial. It originated in the Mediterranean, where it existed first as a leafy plant, without the enlarged root we grow it for these days. Swiss chard, which is a bottomless beet, is an improved version of the early, leafy beets. The modern beet has a round or tapered swollen root—red, yellow, or white—from which sprouts a rosette of large leaves. The leaves as well as the root can be eaten.

How to Plant: Beets can tolerate shade and thrive in well-worked, loose soil that is high in organic matter. They don't like a very acid soil, and they need a lot of potassium.

Beets are grown from seed clusters that are slightly smaller than a pea and contain several seeds each. Plant the clusters an inch deep and an inch apart in rows spaced 12 to 18 inches apart.

Serving Suggestions: Beets are more versatile than they're often given credit for. Eat them raw, or serve the tops raw as a salad green—if you don't cook them, you'll retain some of the vitamins normally lost in cooking. If you cook beets in their skins, the skins will slip off readily at the end of the cooking time.

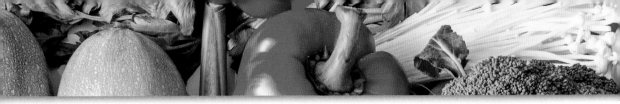

Name: Broccoli

Botanical Name: *Brassica oleracea italica*

Description: This hardy biennial, grown as an annual, is a member of the cabbage or cole family. It looks a bit like a cauliflower that hasn't quite gotten itself together. The flower stalks are green, purple, or white; when it comes to the white-budded ones, the U.S. government has trouble deciding where a broccoli stops and a cauliflower starts. The flowers of all of them are yellow, but they're usually eaten while they're still in bud, before they bloom.

As with other cole family crops, you can grow broccoli in a container on the patio or indoors—a single broccoli plant in an eight-inch flower pot might make a novel house-plant. You can also grow broccoli as an accent in a flower bed.

How to Plant: Broccoli likes fertile, well-drained soil with a pH within the 6.5 to 7.5 range—this discourages disease and lets the plant make the most of the nutrients in the soil. Broccoli is usually grown from transplants except where there's a long cool period, in which case you can sow seed directly in the garden in fall for winter harvest.

Plant transplants that are four to six weeks old with four or five true leaves. If the transplants are leggy or have crooked stems, plant them deeply (up to the first leaves) so they won't grow to be top-heavy. Plant the seedlings 18 to 24 inches apart, in rows 24 to 36 inches apart.

Serving Suggestions: Broccoli is delicious raw, broken into flowerets and used in a salad or with a dipping sauce; the small flowerets are decorative on a platter of raw vegetables. If you've got stalks left over after using the head for salads, parboil them and then sauté them in oil with a little onion and garlic. To make sure the stems cook adequately without overcooking the tender tops, cook broccoli like asparagus—upright in a tall pot so that the stems boil and the tops steam.

Name: Brussels sprouts

Botanical Name: *Brassica oleracea gemmifera*

Description: If you've never seen brussels sprouts outside of a store, you may be quite impressed by the actual plant. Miniature cabbage-like heads, an inch or two in diameter, sprout from a tall, heavy main stem, nestled in among large green leaves. Brussels sprouts belong to the cabbage or cole family and are similar to cabbage in their growing habits and requirements. They're hardy and grow well in fertile soils, and they're easy to grow in the home garden if you follow the correct pest control procedures.

How to Plant: Brussels sprouts like fertile, well-drained soil with a pH within the 6.5 to 7.5 range—this discourages disease and lets the plant make the most of the nutrients in the soil. They're usually grown from transplants, except where there's a long cool period, in which case seeds are sown directly in the garden in fall for winter harvest.

Plant transplants that are four to six weeks old, with four to five true leaves. If the transplants are leggy or have crooked stems, plant them deeply (up to the first leaves) so they won't grow to be top-heavy. Seedlings should be thinned to 24 inches apart when they're three inches tall. If you're planting seeds, set them a half inch deep, three inches apart in rows 24 to 36 inches apart.

Serving Suggestions: Brussels sprouts are traditionally served with turkey at an English Christmas dinner. They're also good lightly steamed and served with a lemon-butter sauce. Don't overcook them; young sprouts should be slightly crunchy, and light cooking preserves their delicate flavor. Older sprouts have a stronger taste.

Name: <u>Cabbage</u>

Botanical Name: *Brassica oleracea capitata*

Description: Cabbage, a hardy biennial grown as an annual, has an enlarged terminal bud made of crowded and expanded overlapping leaves shaped into a head. The leaves are smooth or crinkled in shades of green or purple, and the head can be round, flat, or pointed. The stem is short and stubby, although it may grow to 20 inches if the plant is left to go to seed. Cabbage is a hardy vegetable that grows well in fertile soils, and it's easy to grow in the home garden if you choose suitable varieties and follow correct pest control procedures. Like other mem-

bers of the cabbage or cole family (broccoli and kale are among them), cabbage is a cool-weather crop that can tolerate frost but not heat.

How to Plant: Cabbages like fertile, well-drained soil with a pH within the 6.5 to 7.5 range—this discourages disease and lets the plant make the most of the nutrients in the soil. Cabbages are usually grown from transplants except where there's a long cool period, in which case you can sow seed directly in the garden in fall for winter harvest. Plant transplants that are four to six weeks old with four or five true leaves. If the transplants are leggy or have crooked stems, plant them deeply (up to the first leaves) so they won't grow to be top-heavy. Plant the seedlings 18 to 24 inches apart in rows 24 to 36 inches apart.

Serving Suggestions: Soggy cabbage is a staple of English childhood reminiscences. Actually, steamed or boiled cabbage is an excellent dish—the secret is to cut it into small pieces before you cook it so that it cooks fast and evenly. Or try braising it in a heavy-bottomed pan with butter and just a little water; toss a few caraway seeds over it before serving. Sweet and sour red cabbage is an interesting dish. One way or another, there's a lot more to cabbage than coleslaw.

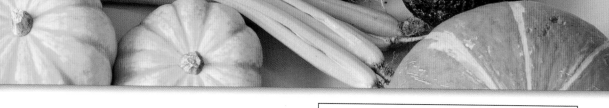

Name: <u>Cardoon</u>

Botanical Name: *Cynara cardunculus*

Description: Cardoon is a tender perennial grown as an annual for its young leaf-stalks, which are blanched and eaten like celery. It looks like a cross between burdock and celery but is actually a member of the artichoke family and has the same deeply cut leaves and heavy, bristled flower head. Cardoon can grow to four feet tall and two feet wide, so it will need plenty of space in your garden.

How to Plant: Transplants should be moved to the garden three to four weeks after the average date of last frost in your area, so if you're growing your transplants from seed you'll need to start them six weeks ahead of your planting date. Cardoon prefers full sun but can tolerate partial shade and grows quickly in any well-drained, fertile soil. Space the young plants 18 to 24 inches apart, with 36 to 48 inches between the rows.

Serving Suggestions: Cut the stalks into sections and parboil them until tender—the time will depend on the size of the stalks. Serve cardoon stalks cut into pieces and chilled with an oil and vinegar dressing, or hot with a cream sauce. Dip chunks into batter and deep-fry them.

Name: <u>Carrots</u>

Botanical Name: *Daucus carota*

Description: Carrots are hardy biennials grown as annuals. They have a rosette of finely divided fernlike leaves growing from a swollen, fleshy taproot. The root, which varies in size and shape, is generally a tapered cylinder that grows up to 10 inches long in different shades of orange. Until the 20th century and the discovery of mechanical refrigeration techniques, root crops like carrots were almost the only vegetables available in the winter. They are cool-weather crops and tolerate the cold; they're easy to grow and have few pest problems, so they're good crops for the home gardener.

How to Plant: Carrots need a cool bed. They prefer full sun but will tolerate partial shade. Before planting, work half a cup of low nitrogen (5–10–10) fertilizer into the soil, and turn the soil thoroughly to a depth of about 10 or 12 inches. This initial preparation is vital for a healthy crop; soil lumps, rocks, or other obstructions in the soil will cause the roots to split, fork, or become deformed.

Sow the seeds in rows 12 to 24 inches apart. Wide-row planting of carrots gives a good yield from a small area.

Serving Suggestions: Carrots fresh from the garden are wonderful raw. Shredded raw carrots are delicious with a touch of oil and lemon; or add raisins and fresh pineapple for an exotic flavor. Add shredded carrots to a peanut butter sandwich. Carrot cake is a staple American confection; try it with a cream cheese frosting. There are any number of ways to cook carrots; perhaps the best treatment for very young fresh carrots is simply to boil them and toss with a respectful touch of butter. You can also try them boiled, then rolled in breadcrumbs and deep-fried, or served with a marmalade glaze.

Name: Cauliflower

Botanical Name: *Brassica oleracea botrytis*

Description: Cauliflower is a single-stalked, half-hardy, biennial member of the cole or cabbage family. It's grown as an annual, and the edible flower buds form a solid head (sometimes called a curd), which may be white, purple, or green. Cauliflowers are prima donnas and need a lot of the gardener's attention. Mark Twain described a cauliflower as a cabbage with a college education.

How to Plant: Cauliflower likes fertile, well-drained soil with a pH within the 6.5 to 7.5 range—this discourages disease and lets the plant make the most of the nutrients in the soil. Like other cole crops, it's usually grown from transplants except where there is a long cool period, in which case you can sow seed directly in the garden in fall for winter harvest. Plant transplants that are four to six weeks old, with four or five true leaves. If the transplants are leggy or have crooked stems, plant them deeply (up to the first leaves) so they won't grow to be top-heavy.

Plant the seedlings 18 to 24 inches apart in rows 24 to 36 inches apart. Plan for only a few heads at a time, or plant seeds and transplants at the same time for succession crops; you'll get the same result by planting early and midseason varieties at the same time. If you're planting seeds, set them half an inch deep and space them three inches apart. Thin them when they're big enough to lift by the true leaves, and transplant the thinned seedlings.

Serving Suggestions: Boil the whole cauliflower head just until the base yields to the touch of a fork. Add lemon juice to the boiling water to preserve the curd's whiteness. Coat the head with a light cheese sauce or simply with melted butter and parsley. Tartar sauce is an original accompaniment to cauliflower, or sprinkle it with browned bread-crumbs for a crunchy texture. Cauliflower pickles are good, too.

Name: <u>Celery</u>

Botanical Name: *Apium graveolens dulce*

Description: Celery is a hardy biennial grown as an annual. It has a tight rosette of eight- to 18-inch stalks, topped with many divided leaves. The flowers look like coarse Queen Anne's lace and are carried on tall stalks. Celery is a more popular vegetable in this country than its cousin celeriac (which it doesn't resemble at all in looks or taste). Both are members of the parsley family, to which dill and fennel also belong, and probably originated in Mediterranean countries.

How to Plant: Celery tolerates light shade and prefers rich soil that is high in organic matter, well able to hold moisture but with good drainage; it does well in wet, almost boggy locations. It's a heavy feeder and needs plenty of fertilizer for continuous quick growth. If you're sowing seeds for transplants, start them two to four months before your estimated planting date—they germinate slowly.

Serving Suggestions: Celery is versatile. You can eat the stems, the leaves, and the seeds. The stems can be boiled, braised, fried, or baked; most people are more accustomed to celery as a raw salad vegetable or relish, but celery is great creamed or baked au gratin. And what could be more elegant than cream of celery soup? The leafy celery tops that most people throw out can be made into a refreshing drink. Boil and strain them, chill the liquid, and drink it by itself or combined with other vegetable juices.

Name: <u>Chard</u>

Botanical Name: *Beta vulgaris cicla*

Description: Chard is basically a beet without the bottom. It's a biennial that's grown as an annual for its big crinkly leaves. Chard is a decorative plant; with its juicy red or white leaf stems and rosette of large, dark green leaves, it can hold its own in the flower garden. It's also a rewarding crop for the home vegetable gardener—it's easy-going and very productive. If you harvest the leaves as they grow, the plant will go on producing all season. Chard has an impressive history, too; it was a popular foodstuff even before the days of the Roman Empire.

How to Plant: Plant chard from seed clusters (which each contain several seeds) about the average date of last frost in your area. Chard tolerates partial shade and likes fertile, well-worked soil with good drainage and a high organic content; like the beet, it is not fond of acid soil. Plant the seed clusters an inch deep and four to six inches apart in rows 18 to 24 inches apart. When they're large enough to handle, thin seedlings to stand about nine to 12 inches apart.

Serving Suggestions: Chard is delicious steamed or cooked like spinach. The leaves have a sweet taste like spinach, and they're colorful in a salad. Chard stalks can be cooked like celery. Cut them into pieces two or three inches long and simmer them until tender; serve them hot with butter or chilled with a light vinaigrette. If you're cooking the leaves and stalks together, give the stalks a five-minute head start so that both will be tender at the end of the cooking time.

Name: <u>Chayote</u>

Botanical Name: *Sechium edule*

Description: The chayote is a tender perennial vine that grows from a tuber and can climb to 30 feet. It's a member of the gourd family, and it has hairy leaves the size and shape of maple leaves; male and female flowers are borne on the same vine. The fruit looks like a greenish or whitish flattened pear. You can eat the young shoots, the fruit, and, if the plant lives long enough, the tubers. Chayote is very popular in Mexico and Central America; it also has a place in American Creole cooking.

How to Plant: You plant the whole fruit with the fat side placed at an angle half way down in the soil so that the stem area is level with the soil surface. The chayote likes well-drained soil with a high content of organic matter and will tolerate partial shade. Space the plants 24 to 30 inches apart, with four or five feet between rows. You don't need to provide a support for the vines unless you want to save space.

Serving Suggestions: Chayote can be prepared any way you prepare squash. Chayote is best eaten young and tender. If it overripens, scoop out the flesh, remove the seed (a large seed, in what looks like a terry cloth bag), mash the flesh with cheese or meat, restuff the empty shell and bake. The tubers of very mature plants are edible and filling, but not very flavorful.

Name: Chick Peas

Botanical Name: *Cicer arietinum*

Description: Chick peas or garbanzos are regarded as beans, but their botanical place is somewhere between the bean and the pea. They're tender annuals and grow on a bushy plant, rather like snap beans but they have a longer growing season. Chick peas have puffy little pods that contain one or two seeds each. In some areas they're grown as a field crop as a food for horses, but they're good food for people, too.

How to Plant: Choose a bed in full sunlight; chick peas tolerate partial shade, but partial shade tends to mean a partial yield. Don't soak the seeds before planting, and don't overwater immediately afterward. Plant seeds an inch deep and two inches apart in rows at least 18 to 24 inches apart. When the seedlings are growing well, thin the plants to four to six inches apart. Cut the seedlings with scissors at ground level; be careful not to disturb the others. They don't mind being a little crowded; in fact, they'll use each other for support.

Serving Suggestions: Shelled chick peas can be steamed or boiled like peas, or roasted like peanuts. Vegetarian cooks often use chick peas with grains as a protein-rich meat substitute. In the Middle East they're puréed with garlic, lemon juice, and spices.

Name: <u>Chicory</u>

Botanical Name: *Cichorium intybus*

Description: Chicory is a hardy perennial with a long, fleshy taproot and a flower stalk that rises from a rosette of leaves. It looks much like a dandelion except that the flowers grow on a branched stalk and are pale blue.

Chicory is grown either for its root, which can be roasted to produce a coffee substitute, or for its tender leaf shoots, which are known as Belgian or blanched endive. This plant is not to be confused with endive or escarole, which are grown as salad greens. Both chicory and endive belong to the same family, and the names are often used inter-changeably, but they aren't the same plant. If you want to produce the chicory root or the Belgian endive, you grow chicory (*Cichorium intybus*)—you can eat the leaves, but that's not why you're growing the variety. If you're growing specifically for greens, you grow endive (*Cichorium endivia*).

Chicory has two stages of development. The first produces the harvestable root. In the second stage, you harvest the root and bury it upright in damp sand or soil until it produces sprouts or heads of pale, blanched leaves; these heads are the Belgian endives. Once you've harvested the heads, you can still use the roots, although they won't be as satisfactory as roots grown specifically for their own sake.

How to Plant: Chicory tolerates partial shade. The soil should be well-drained, high in organic matter, and free of lumps that might cause the roots to fork or split. Plant the seeds an inch deep in rows 24 to 36 inches apart, and thin them to 12 to 18 inches apart when the seedlings are four inches tall.

Serving Suggestions: The roots of chicory are sometimes roasted and ground to add to coffee or used as a coffee substitute. Wash and dice the root, then dry it and roast it before grinding. Blanched endive heads are good braised or in salads.

Name: <u>Chinese Cabbage</u>

Botanical Name: *Brassica chinensis*

Description: Chinese cabbage is a hardy biennial grown as an annual, and it's not a member of the cabbage family. It has broad, thick, tender leaves; heavy midribs; and can be either loosely or tightly headed and grow 15 to 18 inches tall. The variety with a large compact heart is called celery cabbage, pakchoy, or Michihli. In Chinese, call it *pe-tsai*; in Japanese, say *hakusai*. Despite the name, the appearance and taste of Chinese cabbage are closer to lettuce than to regular cabbage.

How to Plant: Chinese cabbage is difficult to grow in the home garden unless you can give it a long, cool growing season. Plant it four to six weeks before your average date of last frost. Even if the first fall frost arrives before the head forms you'll still get a crop of greens. Chinese cabbage will tolerate partial shade. The soil should be well-worked and well-fertilized, high in organic matter and able to hold moisture. Sow seeds in rows 18 to 30 inches apart, and when the seedlings are large enough to handle, thin them to stand eight to 12 inches apart. Don't even attempt to transplant Chinese cabbage unless you've started the seeds in peat pots or other plantable containers.

Serving Suggestions: Chinese cabbage has a very delicate, mild flavor, more reminiscent of lettuce than of cabbage. It makes an interesting slaw, with a sour cream dressing and a little chopped pineapple. Or serve it in wedges like cabbage. Of course, the ideal use is in Chinese stir-fry dishes and soups. Try shredding the Chinese cabbage with a bit of carrot, flavoring it with ginger and soy sauce, and dropping it in spoonfuls into oil in the wok. It's crunchy and delicious.

Name: <u>Collards</u>

Botanical Name: *Brassica oleracea acephalo*

Description: A hardy biennial grown as an annual, the collard grows two to four feet tall and has tufts or rosettes of leaves growing on sturdy stems. Collard is a kind of kale, a primitive member of the cabbage family that does not form a head. The name collard is also given to young cabbage plants that are harvested before they have headed. Collards were England's main winter vegetable for centuries.

How to Plant: Collards like fertile, well-drained soil with a pH within the 6.5 to 7.5 range—this discourages disease and lets the plant make the most of the nutrients in the soil. Collards are usually grown from transplants planted four to six weeks before the average date of last frost, except where there is a long cool period; in this case you can sow seed directly in the garden in fall for a winter harvest.

If you're planting seeds, set them an inch deep and space them three inches apart. Thin them when they're big enough to lift by the true leaves. You can transplant the thinned seedlings. If you're planting transplants, they should be four to six weeks old with four or five true leaves. If the transplants are leggy or have crooked stems, plant them deeply (up to the first leaves) so that they won't grow to be top heavy. Plant the seedlings 12 inches apart in rows 18 to 24 inches apart.

Serving Suggestions: Collards can be steamed or boiled; serve them alone or combine them with ham or salt pork.

90

Name: <u>Corn</u>

Botanical Name: *Zea mays*

Description: Corn, a tender annual that can grow four to 12 feet tall, is a member of the grass family. It produces one to two ears on a stalk, of which only one may be harvestable. The pollen from the tassels must fall into the cornsilk to produce kernels, and if pollination does not occur, all that will grow is the cob. The kernels of sweet corn can be yellow, white, black, red, or a combination of colors.

Despite the popularity of sweet corn and popcorn, most corn is eaten secondhand—the vast majority of the United States corn crop goes into the production of meat. Corn is not the easiest crop to grow in your home vegetable garden, and it doesn't give you a lot of return for the space it occupies. Don't be taken in by all that lush foliage—you will generally get only one harvestable ear of corn from a stalk, although some dwarf varieties will produce two or three.

How to Plant: Corn likes well-worked, fertile soil with good drainage, and it must have full sun. Fertilize the soil before planting, using a third of a pound of a complete, well-balanced fertilizer on each side of a 10-foot row. Place the fertilizer an inch below and two inches away from where you plan to put the seed.

Plant corn when the soil temperature reaches 60°F. Plant the seeds two to four inches apart, in rows (short rows in a block, rather than one long row) or inverted hills. Planting in clumps or blocks ensures pollination. For a continuous supply, plant a dozen seeds of the same variety every two weeks (or when the previous planting shows three leaves), or plant early, midseason, and late varieties at the same time. When the corn is about six inches tall, thin short varieties to two feet apart, tall varieties to three feet apart.

Serving Suggestions: After you've given your homegrown corn all that care and attention—to say nothing of a good deal of your garden space—it is almost unthinkable to do anything with it beyond boiling or steaming it quickly. You can also roast it in the husks in a hot oven or on the barbecue grill. If you have lots, make a delicate corn soup or soufflé.

Name: <u>Cress</u>

Botanical Name: *Lepidium sativum*

Description: Cress is a hardy annual with finely divided tiny green leaves that have a biting flavor. You can grow cress from seed indoors or out—it will even sprout on water-soaked cotton. It takes only 15 to 20 days from planting to harvest, which means more or less instant gratification for the least patient gardener.

Cress has a peppery flavor that gives a lift to salads. There are several kinds available, but the curled variety is the most common.

Other types of cress are upland or winter cress (*Barbarea vernapraecox*) and watercress (*Nasturtium officinale*). Upland or winter cress (*Barbarea vernapraecox*) is a hardy biennial from Europe. You can sow it in the garden in early spring and harvest soon after midsummer.

Watercress is a trailing perennial of European origin with dark green peppery leaves and is usually grown in water. It's easily grown from seed but is usually propagated in temperate climates from stem-pieces, which root easily in wet soil. If you're fortunate enough to have a stream running through your garden, you can try growing watercress on the bank. You can also grow it indoors in pots set in a tray of water. Watercress adds a kick to salads and makes a pretty garnish. It's full of vitamin C and minerals.

How to Plant: When sown outdoors, cress likes well-worked soil with good drainage. It will flourish in shade or semishade and can tolerate a wide range of temperatures. Sow the seeds thickly, a quarter of an inch deep in wide rows, 18 to 24 inches apart, and for a continuous crop repeat the planting every 10 to 14 days.

Serving Suggestions: The English nibble "small salads" of cress and mix the young sprouts with mustard for dainty cress sandwiches. Use it in salads or for a garnish. The peppery taste is a good foil to more bland salad greens.

Name: <u>Cucumbers</u>

Botanical Name: *Cucumis sativus*

Description: Cucumbers are weak-stemmed, tender annuals that can sprawl on the ground or be trained to climb. Both the large leaves and the stems are covered with short hairs; the flowers are yellow. Some plants have both male and female flowers on the same vine, and there may be 10 males to every female flower, but only the female flowers can produce cucumbers. The expression "cool as a cucumber" has long been used to describe a person who is always calm in a crisis, and cucumbers do seem to give off a cool feeling.

How to Plant: Cucumbers will tolerate partial shade, and respond to a rich, well-worked, well-drained soil that is high in organic matter. Plant cucumbers in inverted hills, which you make by removing an inch or two of soil from a circle 12 inches across and using this soil to make a rim around the circle. This protects the young plants from heavy rains that might wash away the soil and leave their shallow roots exposed. Plant six or eight seeds in each hill, and when the seedlings are growing strongly, thin them, leaving the three hardiest plants standing six to 12 inches apart.

Serving Suggestions: Slice cucumbers thinly and dress them with plain yogurt and a little dill. Don't peel them—cucumbers are mostly water anyway, and most of the vitamins they do contain are in the skin. Instead of eating them, you can make them into a refreshing face cleanser—cucumbers are an ingredient in many cosmetic products.

Name: <u>Dandelion</u>

Botanical Name: *Taraxacum officinale*

Description: The dandelion is a hardy perennial that's grown as an annual for its foliage and as a biennial for its roots. The jagged green leaves grow in a short rosette attached by a short stem to a long taproot. Bright yellow flowers one to two inches wide grow on smooth, hollow flower stalks. The dandelion is best known—and feared—by gardeners as a remarkably persistent lawn weed, but its leaves are actually high in vitamin A and four times higher in vitamin C than lettuce. It's also versatile. Dandelion leaves are used raw in salads or boiled like spinach, and the roots can be roasted and made into a coffeelike drink.

How to Plant: Dandelions grow best in a well-drained fertile soil from which you've removed all the stones and rubble. If you're growing dandelions for their foliage only, they'll tolerate soil in poorer physical condition. Plant seeds in the garden a quarter inch deep in rows or wide rows 12 to 18 inches apart. Thin plants six to eight inches apart after the true leaves appear.

Serving Suggestions: Dandelion wine is a brew much beloved of do-it-yourself vintners. Or make dandelion tea, and drink it well-chilled. Remove the stalks from the dandelions and toss the leaves in a vinaigrette dressing. Or try a hot dressing, as for a wilted spinach salad. Cook the leaves quickly and serve them with lemon and oregano, Greek-style. To use the roots, wash and dice them, then dry and roast them before grinding.

Name: <u>Eggplant</u>

Botanical Name: *Solanum melongena*

Description: Eggplant is a very tender perennial plant with large, hairy, grayish-green leaves. The star-shaped flowers are lavender with yellow centers, and the long, slender or round, egg-shaped fruit is creamy-white, yellow, brown, purple, or sometimes almost black. Eggplants will grow two to six feet tall, depending on the variety. They belong to the solanaceous family, are related to tomatoes, potatoes, and peppers, and were first cultivated in India.

How to Plant: You can grow eggplant from seed, but you'll wait 150 days for a harvest. It's easier to grow from transplants, started inside about two months before your outside planting date. Don't put your transplants into the garden until two or three weeks after the average date of last frost for your area—eggplants won't be rushed, and if you plant them too early they won't develop. Eggplants must have full sun. They'll grow in almost any soil, but they do better in rich soil that is high in organic matter, with excellent drainage. Set the plants 18 to 24 inches apart in rows 24 to 36 inches apart.

Serving Suggestions: Eggplant is very versatile and combines happily with all kinds of other foods—cheese, tomatoes, onions, and meats all lend distinction to its flavor. The French use it in a vegetable stew called ratatouille, with tomatoes, onions, peppers, garlic, and herbs. Ratatouille is a good hot side dish or can be served cold as a salad. Eggplant is also a key ingredient of the Greek moussaka, layered with ground meat and topped with a béchamel sauce. Or coat slices in egg and breadcrumbs and deep-fry them. To remove excess moisture from eggplant slices before you cook them, salt them liberally, let them stand about half an hour, wash them, and pat them dry.

Name: <u>Endive</u>

Botanical Name: *Cichorium endivia*

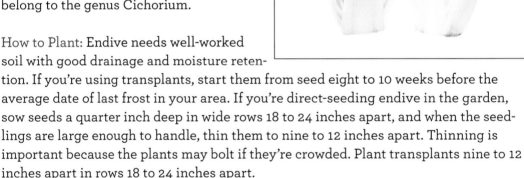

Description: Endive is a half-hardy biennial grown as an annual, and it has a large rosette of toothed curled or wavy leaves that are used in salads as a substitute for lettuce. Endive is often known as escarole, and they're varieties of the same plant; escarole has broader leaves. Endive should not be confused with Belgian endive, which is the young blanched sprout of the chicory plant. Both endive and chicory, however, belong to the genus Cichorium.

How to Plant: Endive needs well-worked soil with good drainage and moisture retention. If you're using transplants, start them from seed eight to 10 weeks before the average date of last frost in your area. If you're direct-seeding endive in the garden, sow seeds a quarter inch deep in wide rows 18 to 24 inches apart, and when the seedlings are large enough to handle, thin them to nine to 12 inches apart. Thinning is important because the plants may bolt if they're crowded. Plant transplants nine to 12 inches apart in rows 18 to 24 inches apart.

Serving Suggestions: Chill endive and serve it with an oil-and-vinegar dressing; add chunks of blue cheese or croutons. Mix it with other salad greens to add a distinctive flavor. The French use endive in a salad with heated slices of mild sausage, diced bacon, and croutons.

Name: Fennel

Botanical Name: *Foeniculum vulgare dulce*

Description: Florence fennel or finocchio is the same as the common or sweet fennel that is grown for use as an herb. The leaves and seeds of both are used the same way for seasoning, but Florence fennel is grown primarily for its bulbous base and leaf stalks, which are used as vegetables. Florence fennel is a member of the parsley family. It's a stocky perennial grown as an annual, and looks rather like celery with very feathery leaves. The plant grows four to five feet tall and has small, golden flowers, which appear in flat-topped clusters from July to September.

How to Plant: Fennel needs well-drained soil that's high in organic matter. Plant the seeds a quarter of an inch deep, in rows two to three feet apart, in full sun. When the seedlings are growing strongly, thin them to 12 inches apart.

Serving Suggestions: Fennel is featured in many Italian dishes. The leaves add flavor to soups and casseroles, and fennel goes well with fish. You can prepare Florence fennel in many ways as you do celery. Cut the fennel stalks into slices, simmer them in water or stock until tender, and serve buttered. Bake slices of fennel with cheese and butter as an accompaniment to a roast, or eat the stalks raw as a dipping vegetable. French and Italian cooks have been using fennel for generations—hence the variety of names by which it's known. The French served grilled sea bass on a bed of flaming fennel stalks, and the dried stalks can be used for barbecuing, too.

Name: <u>Horseradish</u>

Botanical Name: *Armoracia rusticana*

Description: Horseradish looks like a giant, two-foot radish. In fact, it's a hardy perennial member of the cabbage family. Ninety-eight percent of all commercial horseradish is grown in three Illinois counties near St. Louis. Horseradish has a very strong flavor and—like the animal for which it's named—can deliver a powerful kick when you're not expecting it.

How to Plant: Horseradish tolerates partial shade and needs rich, well-drained soil. Turn over the soil to a depth of 10 to 12 inches, and remove stones and lumps that might cause the roots to split. Plant the roots in a trench, and place them 24 inches apart with the narrow end down. Fill in the trench until the thicker end is just covered.

Serving Suggestions: Horseradish is a classic accompaniment to beef roasts and steaks. Serve it solo, freshly grated, to brave souls who appreciate its full flavor. For the less stern of stomach, calm the flavor with whipped or sour cream. Serve it as one of the dipping sauces with a beef fondue. Since the fumes are very strong, grate horseradish outdoors if you can. If you must do it indoors, use a blender.

Name: <u>Jerusalem artichoke</u>

Botanical Name: *Helianthus tuberosus*

Description: Jerusalem artichokes are large, upright, hardy perennials, with small yellow flowers two to three inches across and rough, hairy leaves four to eight inches long. This plant, which grows five to 10 feet tall, was grown by the North American Indians for its tubers, which look like small potatoes. The tubers are low in starch and taste a bit like water chestnuts.

The Jerusalem artichoke isn't an artichoke, and it didn't come from Jerusalem. It's related to the sunflower, and the name is probably derived from the Italian name for a sunflower, girasole, which means turning to the sun.

How to Plant: Give Jerusalem artichokes the least productive soil in your garden (provided the location is sunny); they'll probably love it, and they'll take over areas where nothing else will grow. Plant them as a screen or windbreak. Be sure you know where you want them before you plant, however, because once Jerusalem artichokes become established little short of a tornado will shift them. It's not necessary to fertilize the soil before planting. Plant the tubers two to six inches deep, 12 to 18 inches apart. You won't need to cultivate because weeds are no competition for a healthy Jerusalem artichoke.

Serving Suggestions: The slightly nutty flavor of the Jerusalem artichoke goes well with mushrooms. Serve them cooked until tender then cooled and sliced, in a salad with mushrooms and a vinaigrette dressing. They can also be used raw, peeled, and thinly sliced, in a mushroom salad. Cooked, you can puree them, sauté slices with tomatoes, or simply toss them with butter and seasonings as a side dish with meat or poultry. They can also be used as an extender in meat loaf.

Name: <u>Kale</u>

Botanical Name: *Brassica oleracea acephala*

Description: Kale is a hardy biennial plant grown as an annual. It's a member of the cabbage family and looks like cabbage with a permanent wave. Scotch kale has gray-green leaves that are extremely crumpled and curly; Siberian or blue kale usually is less curly and is a bluer shade of green. There are also decorative forms with lavender and silver variegated leaves.

How to Plant: Kale likes fertile, well-drained soil with pH within the 6.5 to 7.5 range; this discourages disease and lets the plant make the most of the nutrients in the soil. Kale is usually grown from transplants except where there is a long cool period, in which case seed can be sown directly in the garden in fall for winter harvest.

Plant transplants that are four to six weeks old, with four or five true leaves. If the transplants are leggy or have crooked stems, plant them deeply (up to the first leaves) so they won't grow to be top-heavy. Plant the seedlings eight to 12 inches apart, in rows 18 to 24 inches apart.

Serving Suggestions: Young kale makes a distinctive salad green; dress it simply with oil and vinegar. You can also cook it in a little water and serve it with butter, lemon juice, and chopped bacon. Instead of boiling, try preparing it like spinach steamed with butter and only the water that clings to the leaves after washing.

Name: Kohlrabi

Botanical Name: *Brassica caulorapa*

Description: Kohlrabi is a hardy biennial grown as an annual and is a member of the cabbage clan. It has a swollen stem that makes it look like a turnip growing on a cabbage root. This swollen stem can be white, purple, or green, and is topped with a rosette of blue-green leaves. In German, *kohl* means cabbage and *rabi* means turnip—a clue to the taste and texture of kohlrabi, although it is mild and sweeter than either of them. Kohlrabi is a fairly recent addition to the vegetables grown in northern Europe. In this country, nobody paid it any attention until 1800.

How to Plant: Kohlrabi likes fertile, well-drained soil with a pH within the 6.5 to 7.5 range; this discourages disease and lets the plant make the most of the nutrients in the soil. The soil should be high in organic matter. Cole crops are generally grown from transplants except where there's a long cool period. Kohlrabi, however, can be grown directly from seed in the garden. Sow seeds in rows 18 to 24 inches apart and cover them with a quarter to a half inch of soil. When the seedlings are growing well, thin them to five or six inches apart—you can transplant the thinnings. Cultivate carefully to avoid harming the shallow roots.

Serving Suggestions: Small, tender kohlrabi are delicious steamed, without peeling. As they mature you can peel off the outer skin, dice them, and boil them in a little water. Kohlrabi can also be stuffed, like squash.

Try young kohlrabi raw, chilled, and sliced; the flavor is mild and sweet, and the vegetable has a nice, crisp texture. You can also cook kohlrabi, then cut it into strips and marinate the strips in an oil and vinegar dressing; chill this salad to serve with cold cuts. Cooked kohlrabi can be served just with seasoning and a little melted butter or mashed with butter and cream. For a slightly different flavor, cook it in bouillon instead of water.

Name: <u>Leeks</u>

Botanical Name: *Allium porrum*

Description: The leek is a hardy biennial grown as an annual. It's a member of the onion family, but has a stalk rather than a bulb and leaves that are flat and straplike instead of hollow. The Welsh traditionally wear a leek on St. David's Day (March 1) to commemorate King Cadwallader's victory over the Saxons in A.D. 640.

How to Plant: Leeks like a place in full sun and thrive in rich, well-worked soil with good drainage. Plant the seeds an eighth inch deep in rows 12 to 18 inches apart, and thin them six to nine inches apart. To plant transplants, make holes six inches deep, about six to nine inches apart, in well-worked soil. Double rows save space; to make them, stagger the plants with their leaves growing parallel to the rows so they will not grow into the pathway. Drop the leeks in the holes, but do not fill in with rail. Over a period of time, watering will slowly collapse the soil around the leeks and settle them in.

Serving Suggestions: Leeks don't develop bulbs as onions do, but they belong to the same family, and leeks have a delicate onion flavor. Grit and sand get trapped in the wrap-around leaves, so slice the leeks or cut them lengthwise, and wash them thoroughly under running water before you cook them. Serve leeks steamed or braised, chilled in a salad, or in a hot leek and potato soup—keep the soup chunky or puree it for a creamy texture.

Name: Lentils

Botanical Name: *Lens culinaris*

Description: Lentils are a hardy annual member of the pea family. They grow on small weak vines 18 to 24 inches tall, and the small whitish to light purple pealike flowers are followed by flat, two-seeded pods.

How to Plant: Lentils grow best in a sunny area with a fertile well-drained soil. Plant seeds an inch apart and a half inch deep in rows 18 to 24 inches apart. Thin to stand one to two inches apart.

Serving Suggestions: Cooked lentils with a little onion and seasonings, chilled, make a good salad. You can also serve them in a hearty soup; one good soup seasons lentils and tomatoes with thyme and marjoram for a delicate and unusual flavor combination. Try lentils curried with apples and raisins.

Name: <u>Lettuce</u>

Botanical Name: *Lactuca sativa*

Description: Lettuce is a hardy, fast-growing annual with either loose or compactly growing leaves that range in color from light green through reddish-brown. When it bolts, or goes to seed, the flower stalks are two to three feet tall, with small, yellowish flowers on the stalk. The lettuce most commonly found in supermarkets (iceberg or head lettuce) is the most difficult to grow in the home vegetable garden. Butterhead and bibb lettuces, which are often so extravagantly expensive in the store, are easier to grow. Butterhead lettuces have loose heads and delicate crunchy leaves. Stem lettuce (celtuce) might fool you into thinking you're eating hearts of palm and makes a crunchy addition to a salad. Celtuce is grown in the same way as lettuce, except that you want celtuce to bolt or go to seed, because you're going to harvest the thickened stem. You use the leaves of celtuce as you would regular lettuce; the heart of the stem is used like celery.

How to Plant: Lettuce needs well-worked soil with good drainage and moisture retention. Start transplants from seed eight to 10 weeks before your average date of last frost. If you are direct-seeding lettuce in the garden, sow seeds a quarter inch deep in wide rows, and when the seedlings are large enough to handle, thin leaf lettuce to stand six to eight inches apart and head lettuce 12 inches apart.

Serving Suggestions: Yes, salads, of course—but there are other ways to serve lettuce. Braise it in butter with seasoning to taste—the French use nutmeg. Make a wilted salad or cream of lettuce soup, or stir-fry it with mushrooms and onions. Cook peas and shredded lettuce together in a little butter—throw in the lettuce just before you take the peas off the heat. Use several varieties of lettuce together for an interesting combination of shades and textures. Serve a very plain salad—a few leaves of lettuce dressed with oil and a good wine vinegar—to cleanse the palate between courses of a fancy dinner.

Name: <u>Mushrooms</u>

Botanical Name: *Agaricus species*

Description: Mushrooms are the fruiting bodies of a fungus organism, and there are between 60,000 and 100,000 species of fungus that produce mushrooms. Because many mushrooms are poisonous and it's extremely difficult to tell the edible variety from the poisonous kind, gathering wild mushrooms to eat is a very risky pastime. There are, however, many good books on the market that will help you recognize some of the 50 or more edible varieties that grow wild in the United States.

How to Plant: Mushrooms grow best in a dark, humid, cool area. In most homes the best places are the basement and the cabinet under the kitchen sink. A little light won't hurt the mushrooms, but they do need high humidity—80 to 85 percent—and a cool temperature—55° to 60°F.

Mushrooms for growing at home are available in two different forms—in kits or as spawn. You can buy prepared trays and kits already filled with the growing medium and the mushroom spores. All you have to do is remove the tray from the package, add an inch of topsoil, and water. Keep them in a dark, humid, cool place, and you should be harvesting mushrooms within about four weeks.

Serving Suggestions: Fresh mushrooms are wonderful raw, sliced thinly and eaten alone or tossed in a green salad. Simmer them in red wine and tomatoes with parsley and herbs for a delicious vegetarian supper dish. Stuff them with herbed breadcrumbs and broil them, or sauté them lightly and toss them in with a dish of plain vegetables—try them with zucchini. Use mushrooms in your stir-fry dishes; the quick cooking preserves their flavor and texture. You can also fold them into an omelet topped with sherry sauce for an elegant lunch dish.

Name: <u>Muskmelons</u>

Botanical Name: *Cucumis melo*

Description: The muskmelon is a long, trailing annual that belongs to the cucumber and watermelon family. The netted melon or muskmelon is usually called a cantaloupe, but it should not be confused with the real cantaloupe, which is a warty or rock melon. The word cantaloupe means "song of the wolf" and was the name of an Italian castle.

Another type of melon you may like to try in your garden is the honeydew. It's sometimes referred to as a winter melon, but again the name is inaccurate—the true winter melon is a Chinese vegetable. Honeydews have a smoother surface than muskmelons, and lack their distinctive odor. They also ripen later and require a longer growing season, which means that they will not ripen fully in short-season areas.

How to Plant: Muskmelons must have full sun and thrive in well-drained soil that is high in organic matter. Grow muskmelons in inverted hills spaced four to six feet apart. If you're planting from seed, plant six to eight seeds in each hill; when the seedlings have developed three or four true leaves, thin them to leave the strongest two or three seedlings in each hill. Cut the thinned seedlings with scissors at soil level to avoid damaging the survivors' root systems. Where cucumber beetles, other insects, or weather are a problem, wait a bit before making the final selection. If you're using transplants, put two or three in each hill.

Serving Suggestions: Muskmelon or honeydew is delicious by itself. A squeeze of lemon or lime juice brings out the flavor nicely. Or fill the halves with fruit salad, yogurt, or ice cream. You can also scoop out the flesh with a melon-baller, and freeze the balls for future use. Mix balls or chunks of different types of melon for a cool dessert. Serve wedges of honeydew with thinly sliced prosciutto as an appetizer.

Name: Mustard

Botanical Name: *Brassica juncea*

Description: Mustard is a hardy annual with a rosette of large light or dark green crinkled leaves that grow up to three feet in length. The leaves and leaf stalks are eaten. The seeds can be ground and used as a condiment. If you had lived in ancient Rome, you would have eaten mustard to cure your lethargy and any pains you suffered.

How to Plant: Mustard tolerates partial shade and needs well-worked soil, high in organic matter, with good drainage and moisture retention. Plant the seeds half an inch deep in rows 12 to 24 inches apart, and when the seedlings are large enough to handle, thin them to stand six to 12 inches apart. Transplant the thinned seedlings, or eat them in soups or as greens. For a continuous harvest, plant a few seeds at intervals, rather than an entire row at one time. As soon as the plants start to go to seed, pull them up or they will produce a great number of seeds and sow themselves all over the garden. Plant mustard again when the weather begins to cool off.

Serving Suggestions: Use young, tender leaves of mustard in a salad, alone or mixed with other greens. Boil the older leaves quickly in just the water that clings to them after washing; dress them with a little olive oil and vinegar, or add some crumbled bacon. Substitute mustard greens for spinach in an omelette or frittata.

Name: <u>Okra</u>

Botanical Name: *Hibiscus esculentus*

Description: Okra, a member of the cotton and hibiscus family, is an erect, tender annual with hairy stems and large maplelike leaves. It grows from three to six feet tall, and has large flowers that look like yellow hibiscus blossoms with red or purplish centers. When mature, the pods are six to 10 inches long and filled with buckshotlike seeds. Okra is used in Southern cooking, in gumbo or mixed with tomatoes.

How to Plant: Okra will grow in almost any warm, well-drained soil and needs a place in full sun. Plant the seeds a half inch to an inch deep in rows 24 to 36 inches apart, and when the seedlings are growing strongly, thin them to stand 12 to 18 inches apart.

Serving Suggestions: Many people are disappointed because their first mouthful often tastes like buckshot in mucilage. A taste for okra is perhaps an acquired one. Try it in gumbo, mixed with tomatoes, or sautéed.

Name: <u>Onions</u>

Botanical Name: *Allium cepa*

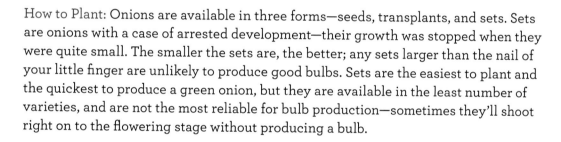

Description: Onions are hardy biennial vegetables usually grown as annuals. They have hollow leaves, the bases of which enlarge to form a bulb. The flower stalk is also hollow, taller than the leaves, and topped with a cluster of white or lavender flowers. The bulbs vary in color from white through yellow to red. All varieties can be eaten as green onions, though spring onions, bunching onions, scallions, and green onions are grown especially for their tops. Green onions take the least time to grow.

How to Plant: Onions are available in three forms—seeds, transplants, and sets. Sets are onions with a case of arrested development—their growth was stopped when they were quite small. The smaller the sets are, the better; any sets larger than the nail of your little finger are unlikely to produce good bulbs. Sets are the easiest to plant and the quickest to produce a green onion, but they are available in the least number of varieties, and are not the most reliable for bulb production—sometimes they'll shoot right on to the flowering stage without producing a bulb.

Onions appreciate a well-made, well-worked bed with all the lumps removed to a depth of at least six inches. When you plant transplants and sets, remember that large transplants and large sets (over three quarters inch in diameter) will often go directly to seed and should be grown only for green or pulling onions. Grow smaller transplants or sets for bulbs. Plant transplants or sets an inch to two inches deep, and two to three inches apart, in rows 12 to 18 inches apart.

Serving Suggestions: Onions are probably the cook's most indispensable vegetable. They add flavor to a huge variety of cooked dishes, and a meat stew or casserole without onions would be a sad thing indeed. Serve small onions parboiled with a cream sauce, or stuff large ones for baking. Serve onion slices baked like scalloped potatoes. Perk up a salad with thin onion rings, or dip thick rings in batter and deep-fry them. Serve onions as one of the vegetables for a tempura. Add chopped, sautéed onion to a cream sauce for vegetables, or fry a big panful of slices to top liver or hamburgers.

Name: Parsnip

Botanical Name: *Pastinaca sativa*

Description: Parsnips are biennials grown as annuals and belong to the same family as celery, carrots, and parsley. A rosette of celerylike leaves grows from the top of the whitish, fleshy root. Parsnips taste like sweet celery hearts. Roman Emperor Tiberius demanded annual supplies of parsnips from Germany. Parsnips were the potato of medieval and Renaissance Europe.

How to Plant: Parsnips prefer full sun but will tolerate partial shade. Plant seeds a half inch deep in wide rows 18 to 24 inches apart. When the seedlings develop two true leaves, thin them to two to four inches apart. Thinning is very important; parsnips must have adequate space for root development. Do not pull out the thinned seedlings; cut them off at ground level to avoid disturbing the remaining seedlings.

Serving Suggestions: Parsnips can be cooked like carrots. If the roots are very large, remove the tough core after cooking. Put parsnips around a beef roast so that they cook in the meat juices, or puree them and add butter and seasonings.

Name: Black-Eyed Peas

Botanical Name: *Gigna sinensis*

Description: Black-eyed peas are tender annuals that can be either bushy or climbing plants, depending on the variety. The seeds of the dwarf varieties are usually white with a dark spot (black eye) where they're attached to the pod; sometimes the spots are brown or purple. Black-eyed peas originated in Asia. Slave traders brought them to Jamaica, where they became a staple of the West Indies' diet.

How to Plant: Black-eyed peas will tolerate partial shade and will grow in very poor soil. In fact, like other legumes, they're often grown to improve the soil. Well-drained, well-worked soil that's high in organic matter increases their productivity. Sow seeds half an inch deep and about two inches apart in rows two to three feet apart; when the seedlings are large enough to handle, thin them to three or four inches apart.

Serving Suggestions: Eat young black-eyed peas in the pod like snap beans; dry the shelled peas for use in casseroles and soups. Combine cooked black-eyed peas and rice, season with red pepper sauce, and bake until hot; or simmer the peas with pork or bacon for a classic Southern dish.

Name: <u>Peas</u>

Botanical Name: *Pisum sativum*

Description: Peas are hardy, weak-stemmed, climbing annuals that have leaf-like stipules, leaves with one to three pairs of leaflets, and tendrils that they use for climbing. The flowers are white, streaked, or colored. The fruit is a pod containing four to 10 seeds, either smooth or wrinkled depending on the variety. Custom has it that you can make a wish if you find a pea pod with nine or more peas in it.

Edible-pod peas are a fairly recent development. Grow them the same way as sweet peas, but harvest the immature pod before the peas have developed to full size. Peas have traditionally been a difficult crop for the home gardener to grow, with yields so low that it was hardly worth planting them. All you need to grow peas is cool weather and a six-foot support trellis.

How to Plant: Peas tolerate partial shade and need good drainage in soil that is high in organic material. They produce earlier in sandy soil, but yield a heavier, later crop if grown in clay soil. Although soaking seeds can speed germination, a lot of seed can be ruined by oversoaking, and peas are harder to plant when they're wet, because the seeds tend to break. Plant the peas two inches deep, one to two inches apart, in rows 18 to 24 inches apart.

Serving Suggestions: Freshly shelled peas are a luxury seldom enjoyed by most people. Cook them quickly in a little water and serve them with butter and chopped mint. Or add a sprig of mint during cooking. Fresh peas and boiled new potatoes are the perfect accompaniment for a lamb roast. Add edible pod peas to a stir-fry dish—the rapid cooking preserves their crisp texture and delicate flavor. Eat them raw, or use them alone, lightly steamed, as a side dish.

Name: <u>Peanuts</u>

Botanical Name: *Arachis hypogaea*

Description: The peanut is a tender annual belonging to the pea family. It grows
six inches to 2 1/2 feet tall, depending on
whether it's the bunch type, which grows
upright, or the runner type, which spreads
out over the ground. Small clusters of
yellow, sweet-pea-like flowers grow on
stems called pegs. The pegs grow down
and push into the soil, and the nuts develop from them one to three inches underground. You can grow a peanut plant
indoors if you give it lots of sunlight; it's a
novel and entertaining houseplant.

How to Plant: Peanuts like well-worked sandy soil that is high in organic matter. The
pegs have difficulty penetrating a heavy clay soil. Plant either shelled raw peanuts or
transplants six to eight inches apart, in rows 12 to 18 inches apart. If you're growing
from seed, plant the seeds one to three inches deep. Grow them in double rows to
save space.

Serving Suggestions: You probably won't be able to resist eating your peanuts as
snacks, but if you've got lots, make peanut butter. Run the nuts through a meat grinder
for crunchy peanut butter; for the smooth kind put them in the blender. And imagine
homemade peanut butter cookies with homegrown peanuts—you'll be one up on
everyone at the school bazaar. Add peanuts and candied orange peel to a fudge recipe—
it makes a delicious crunchy candy.

Name: <u>Peppers</u>

Botanical Name: *Capsicum frutescens* (hot pepper); *Capsicum annuum* (sweet and hot peppers)

Description: Peppers are tender erect perennials that are grown as annuals. They have several flowers growing in the angle between the leaf and stem. Sweet peppers are erect annuals that have only a single flower growing from the space between the leaf and the stem.

Peppers range in size from the large sweet bullnose or mango peppers to the tiny, fiery bird or devil peppers. Peppers also grow in many shapes: round, long, flat, and twisted. Some like them hot, some like them sweet. The large sweet ones are used raw, cooked, or pickled, and the hot ones are used as an unmistakable favoring or relish.

How to Plant: Peppers do best in a soil that is high in organic matter and that holds water but drains well. Plant the pepper transplants in full sun, 18 to 24 inches apart, in rows 24 to 36 inches apart.

Serving Suggestions: Stuffed, raw, pickled, or roasted, sweet and hot peppers add lively flavor to any meal. Stuff sweet peppers with tuna, chicken, a rice and meat mixture, or chili con carne. For a vegetarian dish, stuff them with rice and chopped vegetables, a cheese mixture, or seasoned breadcrumbs. Stuff raw peppers with cream cheese, slice into rings, and serve in a salad. Use thick rings in a dish of vegetables for tempura. Use chopped peppers in chili and spaghetti sauce recipes, and add a spoonful of chopped hot pepper to a creamy corn soup for an interesting flavor contrast.

When you're preparing raw hot peppers, cut and wash them under running water and wash your hands well when you're finished. Avoid rubbing your eyes while handling hot peppers. Milk is more soothing than water for washing the hot pepper's sting from your skin.

Name: <u>Potatoes</u>

Botanical Name: *Solanum tuberosum*

Description: The potato is a perennial grown as an annual. It's a weak-stemmed plant with hairy, dark green compound leaves that look a little like tomato leaves, and it produces underground stem tubers when mature. The potato is a member of the solanaceous family, and is related to the tomato, the eggplant, and the pepper; it originated at high altitudes and still prefers cool nights.

How to Plant: Potatoes are grown from whole potatoes or pieces of potatoes—these are called seed pieces; each piece must have at least one eye. Always plant certified disease-free seed pieces, and don't try to use supermarket potatoes, which have been chemically treated to prevent sprouting.

Potatoes need well-drained fertile soil, high in organic matter, with pH of 5.0 to 5.5. Adding lime to improve the soil and reduce acidity usually increases the size of the crop, but it also increases the incidence of scab—a condition that affects the skin of the potato but not the eating quality. Plant potatoes or potato pieces in full sun, four inches deep, 12 to 18 inches apart, in rows 24 to 36 inches apart.

Serving Suggestions: Potatoes are wonderfully versatile in the kitchen—you can boil, bake, roast, fry, puree, sauté, and stuff them. The enterprising cook can serve a different potato dish every day for a month. Small new potatoes are delicious boiled and tossed in butter and parsley or mint; don't peel them. Stuff potatoes with tuna and spinach for a nourishing all-in-one dish. Enjoy low-calorie fries by brushing the fries all over with oil and baking them in a single layer on a cookie sheet. Don't throw away potato skins—they're full of goodness.

A nonedible use for potatoes: Cut a potato in half, and carve a picture or design on the cut surface; ink it, and press on paper for an instant block print.

Name: <u>Pumpkins</u>

Botanical Name: *Cucurbita maxima*; *Cucurbita moschata*; *Cucurbita pepo*

Description: Pumpkins are tender annuals with large leaves on branching vines that can grow 20 feet long. The male and female flowers—sometimes as large as eight inches in diameter—grow on the same vine, and the fruit can weigh as much as 100 pounds. The name pumpkin is also given to a number of other squashes and gourds—anything that's orange and hard. The harvest poem reference, "when the frost is on the pumpkin," means the first light frost, not

a hard freeze. The first pumpkin pies were made by pouring milk into a pumpkin and baking it.

How to Plant: Pumpkins can tolerate partial shade and prefer well-drained soil, high in organic matter. Too much fertilizer tends to encourage the growth of the vines rather than the production of pumpkins. Plant pumpkins in inverted hills, made by removing an-inch of soil from a circle 12 inches in diameter and using the soil to build up a rim around the circle; leave six feet between hills. Plant six to eight seeds in each hill, and thin to two or three when the seedlings appear. When the seedlings have four to six true leaves, thin to only one plant in each hill. Cut off the thinned seedlings at soil level to avoid disturbing the roots of the chosen survivor. One early fruit can suppress the production of any more pumpkins. Some people suggest removing this first pumpkin, but this is a gamble because there's no guarantee that others will set. If you remove it, eat it like squash.

Serving Suggestions: Spice up the cooked pumpkin flesh for pie fillings, breads, or muffins; or use it in custards, or as a stuffing for meats or vegetables. Roast the seeds for a nutritious snack. If a pumpkin has served only briefly as a jack-o'-lantern, you can still use the flesh for cooking.

Name: Radishes

Botanical Name: *Raphanus sativus* (spring radish); *Raphanus sativus longipinnatus* (winter radish)

Description: Radishes are hardy annuals or biennials that produce white, red, or black roots and stems under a rosette of lobed leaves. They're fun to grow, and youngsters get hooked on gardening after growing radishes more than any other vegetable. A bunch of radishes, well washed, makes a great posy to give away. Radishes are distantly related to horseradish.

How to Plant: Radishes tolerate partial shade and like well-worked, well-drained soil. If you're planting winter radishes, be sure to loosen the soil well and remove soil lumps or rocks that might cause the roots to become deformed. Plant seeds half an inch deep in rows or wide rows 12 to 18 inches apart.

Serving Suggestions: Radishes can be sculptured into rosettes or just sliced into a salad. They are low in calories and make good cookie substitutes when you have to nibble. Put radishes on a relish tray, or on a platter of vegetables for dipping. Try "pickling" the excess crop by mincing them and marinating in vinegar.

Name: <u>Rhubarb</u>

Botanical Name: *Rheum rhaponticum*

Description: A hardy perennial, rhubarb grows two to four feet tall, with large, attractive leaves on strong stalks. The leaf stalks are red or green and grow up from a rhizome or underground stem, and the flowers are small and grow on top of a flower stalk. Don't allow the plant to reach the flowering stage; remove the flower stalk when it first appears. You eat only the rhubarb stalks; the leaves contain a toxic substance and are not for eating.

How to Plant: Rhubarb likes rich, well-worked soil that is high in organic matter and drains well. Give it a place in full sun or light shade. Plant the divisions about three feet apart in rows three to four feet apart, with the growing tips slightly below the soil surface.

Serving Suggestions: Botanically, rhubarb is a vegetable, but for culinary purposes it is a fruit. It's good in pies, jams, and jellies, and can be eaten baked or stewed as a topping for a cooked breakfast cereal. It has a tart taste and needs to have sugar added. The sweetened juice makes a refreshing cold drink. Add finely chopped rhubarb to any nut bread recipe.

Name: <u>Rutabaga</u>

Botanical Name: *Brassica napobrassica*

Description: Rutabaga is a hardy biennial grown as an annual. It has a rosette of smooth, grayish-green leaves that grow from the swollen stem, and it has a root that can be yellow, purple, or white. The rutabaga can be distinguished from the turnip by the leaf scars on its top, and the leaves are more deeply lobed than the turnip's. As vegetables go, rutabagas are a fairly modern invention. They were created less than 200 years ago by crossing a cabbage with a turnip.

How to Plant: Rutabagas do best in well-drained soil that's high in organic matter. Although they're less likely than carrots to fork or split, they need well-worked soil with all the rocks and soil lumps removed. Plant the seeds half an inch deep in rows 18 to 24 inches apart, and when the seedlings are large enough to handle, thin them to six to eight inches apart. Thinning is important; like all root crops, rutabagas must have room to develop.

Serving Suggestions: Peel rutabagas and steam or boil until tender; then mash them for use in puddings and pancakes. They can also be served sliced or diced. Add rutabagas to vegetable soups and stews. Sauté them in butter with apples and brown sugar. Rutabaga is very good with lots of butter or sour cream; low-calorie alternatives are yogurt or low-fat cream cheese.

Name: <u>Salsify</u>

Botanical Name: *Tragopogon porrifolius*

Description: Salsify is a hardy biennial grown as an annual. It's related to dandelion and chicory, and its flowers look like lavender chicory blossoms. The edible part is the long taproot. This salsify should not be confused with black salsify (*Scorzonera hispanica*) or Spanish salsify (*Scolymus hispanicus*); both of these are related to the radish. Some people claim that salsify has a slight oyster flavor—hence the name "oyster plant." It tastes rather like artichoke hearts.

How to Plant: Plant salsify seeds in full sun in rich, well-worked soil. Work the soil thoroughly to a depth of eight to 12 inches, and remove all stones, soil lumps, or rocks that might cause the roots to fork and split. Plant the seeds half an inch deep in rows 18 to 24 inches apart, and when the seedlings are large enough to handle, thin them to stand two to four inches apart.

Serving Suggestions: Salsify roots should not be peeled before cooking; they can "bleed." Scrub them clean, steam, and slice them, then dip the slices in batter or breadcrumbs and fry; serve with tartar sauce. People who have never had oysters can't tell them apart. Try salsify braised with lemon and butter—the lemon helps preserve the color. Or serve it with a white sauce; add chopped parole parsley for color.

Name: <u>Shallots</u>

Botanical Name: *Allium cepa*

Description: The shallot is a very hardy biennial grown as an annual, and it's a member of the onion family. It's believed that French knights returning from the Crusades introduced them to Europe, and that De Soto brought them to America in 1532. Shallot plants grow about eight inches tall in a clump, with narrow green leaves, and look very much like small onions; they're favorites with gourmets. The roots are very shallow and fibrous, and the bulbs are about a half inch in diameter when mature. The small bulbs have a more delicate flavor than regular onions. Use the young outer leaves like chives.

How to Plant: Shallots can be grown in any soil but may have less flavor when they're grown in clay soils. Shallots are very shallow-rooted plants and need little soil preparation. Although they prefer full sun, they'll survive in partial shade. Shallots seldom form seed, so they're usually grown from cloves, which should be planted four to six weeks before your average date of last frost. Plant the cloves six to eight inches apart in rows 12 inches apart, and set them so that the tops of the cloves are even with the soil, but no deeper. Keep them carefully cultivated when they're small; the shallow root systems don't like to compete with weeds.

Serving Suggestions: Shallots have a delicate flavor and are less overpowering than many onions. They're very good stirred into sour cream as a dressing for vegetables or fish, or chopped and added to an oil-and-vinegar dressing for salads. Use the small bulbs in the classic French beef stew, *boeuf bourguignon*.

Name: Sorrel

Botanical Name: *Rumex acetosa*; *Rumex patientia*; *Rumex scutatus*; *Rumex abyssinicus*

Description: Several varieties of sorrel will do well in your garden. Garden sorrel (*R. acetosa*) grows about three feet tall and produces leaves that are good used fresh in salads; herb patience or spinach dock (*R. patientia* is a much taller plant, with leaves that can be used either fresh or cooked. French sorrel (*R. scutatus*) grows only six to 12 inches tall; its fiddle-shaped leaves make good salad greens. Spinach rhubarb (*R. abyssinicus*) is a lofty plant—it grows up to eight feet tall. As the name suggests, you can cook the leaves like spinach and the stalks like rhubarb. Avoid other varieties—they're weeds and not good for eating.

How to Plant: All the sorrels require a sunny location with well-drained, fertile soil. Plant sorrels from seed two to three weeks before the average date of last frost. Plant the seeds a half inch deep in rows 18 to 24 inches apart, and when the plants are six to eight weeks old, thin them to 12 to 18 inches apart.

Serving Suggestions: You can use sorrel leaves raw, as salad greens or very lightly steamed or boiled and tossed in butter. Sorrel soup is a classic French favorite, and the Russians use sorrel in a green borscht soup. In the time of Henry VIII, sorrel was used as a spice and to tenderize meat. The English also mashed the leaves with vinegar and sugar as a dressing for meat and fish—hence the name green sauce.

Name: <u>Soybeans</u>

Botanical Name: *Glycine max*

Description: The soybean is a tender, free-branching annual legume. Though it can grow five feet tall, it's usually only two to 3½ feet tall. The stems and leaves are hairy; the flowers are white with lavender shading, and the pods are one to four inches long and grow in clusters. The soybean is extremely high in protein and calcium and is a staple of a vegetarian diet. It's also very versatile and can be used to make milk, oil, tofu, or a meat substitute.

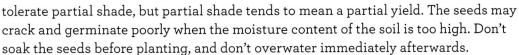

How to Plant: After the last frost is over, choose a bed in full sunlight; soybeans tolerate partial shade, but partial shade tends to mean a partial yield. The seeds may crack and germinate poorly when the moisture content of the soil is too high. Don't soak the seeds before planting, and don't overwater immediately afterwards.

Plant seeds an inch deep, one to two inches apart in rows 24 to 30 inches apart. When the seedlings are growing well, thin the plants to two inches apart. Cut the seedlings with scissors at ground level; be careful not to disturb the others. Soybeans don't mind being a little crowded; in fact, they'll use each other for support.

Serving Suggestions: The Japanese cook soybeans in salted water, serve them in the shell, and then squeeze out the seeds and eat them. Soybeans are extremely versatile; they can be made into oil, milk, or tofu—a major foodstuff among vegetarians. Soybeans are also used as a high-protein meat substitute or ground into flour. Soybeans supply about half the vegetable fats and oils used in this country.

Name: Spinach

Botanical Name: *Spinacia oleracea*

Description: There are two kinds of spinach—the regular kind which is a hardy annual, and the less well-known New Zealand spinach, which is a tender annual and is not really spinach at all. Spinach, the regular kind, is a hardy annual with a rosette of dark green leaves. The leaves may be crinkled (savoy leaf) or flat. Spinach is related to beets and chard. The cartoon character Popeye made spinach famous with young children because he attributed his great strength to eating spinach—probably with some justification, because spinach has a very high iron content.

How to Plant: Both spinach and New Zealand spinach are grown—like beets and chard— from seed clusters that each produce several seedlings. This means they must be thinned when the seedlings appear. Both types tolerate partial shade and require well-drained soil that's rich in organic matter. Spinach does not like acid soil. Plant spinach seed clusters half an inch deep, two to four inches apart, in rows 12 to 14 inches apart.

For New Zealand spinach, plant the seed clusters half an inch deep, 12 inches apart, in rows 24 to 36 inches apart.

Serving Suggestions: Both spinach and New Zealand spinach can be used in the same ways, and the following suggestions apply to both. Fresh spinach is wonderful in salads, and its dark green leaves add color and variety to lettuce. Add orange segments and almonds to a salad of fresh spinach, and toss in a sweet-sour dressing. Add cubes of cheese to spinach, peppers, and sliced fresh mushrooms for an appealing lunchtime salad. Children who hate cooked spinach on principle often enjoy it raw. Spinach is an attractive ingredient for a quiche; add flaked salmon for a more substantial meal.

Name: <u>Summer Squash</u>

Botanical Name: *Cucurbita species*

Description: The cucumber family, to which squashes belong, probably has the greatest diversity of shapes and sizes of any vegetable family except the cabbages. It's the genus Cucurbita and includes certain gourds and pumpkins, as well as squashes. Summer squashes are eaten when they are immature; winter squashes are eaten when mature.

Squashes are hard to confine. A bush-type zucchini will grow well in a tire planter if kept well-watered and fertilized; a vining squash can be trained up a fence. Summer squashes are weak-stemmed, tender annuals, with large, cucumberlike leaves and separate male and female flowers that appear on the same plant. Summer squash usually grows as a bush, rather than as a vine; the fruits have thin, tender skin and are generally eaten in the immature stage before the skin hardens. The most popular of the many kinds of summer squashes are crookneck, straightneck, scallop, and zucchini.

How to Plant: Squash varieties like well-worked soil with good drainage. They're heavy feeders, so the soil must be well fertilized. Two to three weeks after your area's average date of last frost, when the soil is warm, plant squash in inverted hills. Make inverted hills by removing an inch of soil from an area about 12 inches across and using this soil to form a ring around the circle.

Serving Suggestions: Summer squashes lend themselves to a good variety of culinary treatments. Sauté slices of summer squash with onions and tomatoes for a robust but delicately flavored side dish. Add sliced zucchini and mushrooms to a thick tomato sauce for spaghetti. Halve summer squashes and stuff with a meat or rice mixture, or bake them with butter and Parmesan cheese. Panfry slices of summer squash, or simmer them with fruit juice for a new flavor. Use the popular zucchini raw on a relish tray and among vegetables for a tempura, or slice it thinly in salads. Use the larger fruits for making zucchini bread.

Name: <u>Winter Squash</u>

Botanical Name: *Cucurbita species*

Description: The cucumber family, to which squashes belong, probably has the greatest diversity of shapes and sizes of any vegetable family, except the cabbages. It's the genus *Cucurbita*, and includes certain gourds, and pumpkins, as well as squashes. Most are trailing or climbing plants with large yellow flowers (both male and female); the mature fruits have a thick skin and a definite seed cavity. "Summer squash," "winter squash" and "pumpkin" are not definite botanical names. "Pumpkin," which any child can tell you is a large vegetable used for jack-o'-lanterns and pies, is applied to long-keeping varieties of *C. moschata*, *C. pepo*, and a few varieties of *C. maxima*. Summer squashes are eaten when they are immature; winter squashes are eaten when mature. Squashes are hard to confine. A bush-type squash will grow well in a tire planter if kept well-watered and fertilized; a vining squash can be trained up a fence.

How to Plant: Squash varieties like well-worked soil with good drainage. They're heavy feeders, so the soil must be well-fertilized, Two to three weeks after your area's average date of last frost, when the soil is warm, plant squash in inverted hills. Make inverted hills by removing an inch of soil from an area about 12 inches across and using this soil to form a ring around the circle. Make the inverted hills three to four feet apart, and plant four or five seeds in each one. When the seedlings are large enough to handle, thin them to leave the two or three strongest young plants standing. Cut the thinned seedlings off at soil level with scissors; if you pull them out you'll disturb the roots of the remaining seedlings.

Serving Suggestions: Winter squashes lend themselves to a good variety of culinary treatments and have the flexibility of adapting to both sweet and savory uses. Cut winter squashes into halves and bake them; serve them with honey or brown sugar and butter. Fill the halves with browned sausages, or mash the pulp and season well with salt and pepper. As a treat for the children, top mashed squash with marshmallow and brown it under the grill. Use the pulp of winter squash as a pie filling—it makes a pleasant change from pumpkin.

Name: <u>Sweet Potatoes</u>

Botanical Name: *Ipomoea batatas*

Description: The sweet potato is a tender vining or semi-erect perennial plant related to the morning glory. It has small white, pink, or red-purple flowers and swollen, fleshy tubers that range in color from creamy-yellow to deep red-orange. There are "dry" and "moist" kinds of sweet potatoes, which describes the texture when they're eaten; some dry varieties have a higher moisture content than some moist ones. The moist varieties are often called yams, but the yam is actually a different species that is found in tropical countries. Sweet potato vines are ornamental, so this vegetable is often grown as ground cover or in planters or hanging baskets. You can even grow a plant in water in your kitchen—suspend the sweet potato on toothpicks in a jar of water, and watch it grow.

How to Plant: Sweet potatoes are planted from rooted sprouts, or slips, taken from a mature tuber. To grow your own slips, place several sweet potato roots about an inch apart in a hotbed and cover with two inches of sand or light soil. Add another inch of soil when the shoots appear, keep the bed at a temperature between 70° and 80°F, and don't let it dry out. In about six weeks you will have rooted slips that can be planted in the garden.

A good, sandy soil is best for sweet potatoes. Over-rich soil produces luxuriant vines but small tubers. The soil should be moderately fertile, rich in organic matter, and well-worked to ensure looseness. For good tuber production sweet potatoes must have full sun; in partial shade the vine will be handsome but not very productive. Set the slips on ridges made by mounding up the soil about eight inches high along rows three feet apart. Make the ridges about 12 inches wide, and set the slips at 12-inch intervals.

Serving Suggestions: Sweet potatoes are very versatile; you can boil, steam, fry, or bake them, and they take well to either sweet or savory seasoning. Use pureed sweet potatoes in bread or cookies. Candy them, or stuff them and bake them in their skins. Include slices of raw sweet potato with the vegetables for a tempura. Cinnamon, cloves, nutmeg, and allspice all go well with sweet potatoes.

Name: <u>Tomatoes</u>

Botanical Name: *Lycopersicon esculentum*

Description: Tomatoes are tender perennials grown as annuals. They have weak stems and alternate lobed and toothed leaves that have a distinctive odor. The yellow flowers grow in clusters. Most tomatoes have vining growth habits and need a fair amount of space. Some are advertised as bush varieties that save space, but they'll still sprawl if you let them, and you may still have to stake or cage them.

Tomatoes can be divided into two main groups, according to growth habits: determinate and indeterminate. On the determinate tomato (bush tomato), the plant stops growing when the end buds set fruit—usually at about three feet tall. It seldom needs staking. On the indeterminate tomato (vine tomato), the end buds do not set fruit; the plant can grow almost indefinitely if not stopped by frost. Most of the varieties that are staked or caged are indeterminate tomatoes.

How to Plant: Tomatoes must have full sun and need warm, well-drained, fertile soil. Although they will produce earlier in sandy soils, they will have a larger yield in clay soils. Plant seeds half an inch deep in rows 24 to 48 inches apart (depending on how large the variety will grow).

Serving Suggestions: Fresh tomatoes from your garden are wonderful with very little embellishment—slice them, and dress them with a touch of olive oil and lemon juice and a pinch of basil; or eat them as fruit with a little sugar. Alternate slices of fresh tomato and cooked potato for an interesting side dish—add olive oil and parsley. Add tomatoes to almost any salad, or serve them alone, sliced with bread and cheese for an instant lunch.

Name: <u>Turnip</u>

Botanical Name: *Brassica rapa*

Description: The turnip, a hardy biennial grown as an annual, sports a rosette of hairy, bright green leaves growing from a root—which is not really a root, but a swelling at the base of the stem. The turnip is more commonly grown for use as a root vegetable, but can also be grown for the leaves, which are used as greens. Turnips originated in the Mediterranean in prehistoric times. The rutabaga, a younger cousin, is believed to have come about in the Middle Ages from a cross between a turnip and a cabbage. Englishmen have been known to refer to each other as "turniphead"; this is not a compliment, as turnips are often considered to be rather dull. In fact, they're quite versatile.

How to Plant: Turnips tolerate partial shade and need soil that's high in organic matter and well-drained but able to hold moisture. Too much nitrogen in the soil encourages the plant to produce leaves and a seed stalk rather than a good-sized root, so when you're preparing the soil for planting, work in a low-nitrogen fertilizer. Plant seeds half an inch deep in rows or wide rows 12 to 24 inches apart.

Serving Suggestions: When small, turnips make a great substitute for radishes. They're also easier to carve than radishes if you feel the urge to sculpture roses or daisies for decorative garnishes. Sliced raw turnips give a nice crunch to salads. Steam or boil turnips and serve them with butter or cream—add a little sugar to the cooking water to improve the flavor. They're very good in soups or stews or cooked around a roast. You can use the tops in a salad or cooked as greens.

Name: <u>Watermelons</u>

Botanical Name: *Citrullus vulgaris*

Description: The watermelon is a spreading, tender annual vine related to the cucumber. It produces round, oval, or oblong fruits that can weigh five to 100 pounds and have pink, red, yellow, or greyish-white flesh. Male and female flowers appear on the same vine. Although smaller varieties are now available, you still need to give watermelons a lot of headroom. They're space-consuming, and they take a lot of nutrients from the soil, so they're still not the ideal crop for some gardens.

How to Plant: Watermelons must have full sun, and prefer well-drained soil that holds moisture well. Grow watermelons in inverted hills, made by removing an inch of soil from a circle 12 inches across and using the soil to form a rim around the circle. Space the hills six feet apart, and plant four to five seeds in each hill. When the seedlings have developed three or four true leaves, thin them to leave the strongest one or two seedlings in each hill. Cut the thinned seedlings with scissors at soil level to avoid damaging the survivors' root systems. Where cucumber beetles, other insects, or weather are a problem, wait a bit before making the final selection. If you're using transplants, put two or three in each hill.

Serving Suggestions: Slices of fresh watermelon make a wonderful summer cooler. Scoop out the flesh with a melon baller and add to other types of melon for a cool fruit salad—pile the fruit into a muskmelon half. For a great party dish, serve a big fruit salad in the scooped out half-shell of the watermelon—or carve the shell into a basket. Make pickles with the rind.

CHAPTER 8: HERB PROFILES

Name: <u>Aloe</u>

Botanical Name: *Aloe vera* or *A. barbadensis*

Description: Aloe vera is the most common of the more than 300 species of aloe. Resistant to salt and drought, this very hardy herb can be found on rocky shorelines or dunes or intermingled with other vegetation just about anywhere. A common houseplant, aloe is characterized by pointed, fleshy leaves that exude a mucilaginous (gelatin-like) sap when broken. Aloe produces yellow to orange-red tubular flowers that grow to 1 inch.

How to Plant: Aloe needs neutral, average, well-drained soil with filtered sun to shade. In good soil and a warm climate, an aloe plant will thrive for years.

Aloe's tiny black seeds can germinate in about four weeks but often take many months. The best way to obtain new plants is to remove suckers or offshoots from the mother plant when they have grown 1 to 2 inches for an indoor plant and 6 to 8 inches for an outdoor plant. The herb takes two to three years to flower. Aloe is sold in nurseries throughout the country.

Uses: This common plant has many uncommon virtues. Cleopatra is said to have massaged fresh aloe gel into her skin every day to preserve her beauty. Modern clinical studies show that aloe is one of the best herbs for soothing skin and healing burns, rashes, frostbite, and severe wounds. It is also used to treat eczema, dandruff, acne, ringworm, gum disease, and poison oak and ivy. Aloe is found commercially in a number of creams and lotions for softening and moisturizing skin. It works by inhibiting formation of tissue-injuring compounds that gather at the site of a skin injury.

Name: <u>Angelica</u>

Botanical Name: *Angelica archangelica*

Description: This large, boldly attractive plant produces lush growth, making it a striking focal point for your garden. Angelica looks much like a very large celery or parsnip plant. This herb produces large white umbel flower heads and decorative yellow-green seedpods. Often you'll find angelica growing near seas, streams, and mountain brooks and in marshes, swamps, and moist meadows. It is native to Syria and possibly Europe but now cultivated elsewhere, including the United States.

How to Plant: Angelica likes a cool, moist location and average to well-drained soil. It will grow in sun but prefers partial shade.

Seeds must be no more than 6 months old to germinate. Sow them in late fall. Scatter seeds on top of soil and lightly cover with additional soil. Plant seeds directly in the garden, or transplant seedlings. Mature angelica plants do not like to be moved.

Uses: For centuries, people gathered angelica to ward off evil spirits. Early physicians prescribed angelica for a number of illnesses. Angelica syrup was taken as a digestive aid, and American Indians used angelica to treat lung congestion. Today angelica is used primarily to treat digestive and bronchial conditions and as an expectorant and cough suppressant. It has antibacterial, antifungal, and diaphoretic (induces sweating) properties. It also increases menstrual flow. Studies have shown that compounds from Chinese angelica may also have cancer-fighting properties.

Commercially, angelica roots and seeds are used to flavor Benedictine and Chartreuse liqueurs, gin, vermouth, and some brands of tobacco. The herb's distinctive flavor is also found in fresh or dried leaves and stems. Add very small amounts of fresh leaves to salads, fruits, soups, stews, desserts, and pastries.

Name: <u>Anise</u>

Botanical Name: *Pimpinella anisum*

Description: Anise produces feathery leaves and a lacy flower umbel on slender, weak stems. The plant strongly resembles dill. It is native to Egypt and the Mediterranean region and widely cultivated in Europe, India, Mexico, Russia, and the United States.

How to Plant: Anise prefers full sun and average, light, dry soil. Sow seed in the garden, or transplant seedlings when small. Like dill, anise grows best in rows or clumps so its weak multiple stems can support one another. It takes at least four months of warm, frost-free weather to grow seeds to maturity. In northern areas, the growing season is usually not long enough for anise to produce seeds.

Sow seed in early spring. Because the plant produces a long taproot, it is difficult to transplant.

Uses: Anise has been considered a valuable herb since at least the 6th century BC. The Romans cultivated the plant for its distinctive fragrance and flavor, which is similar to licorice. They also used anise extensively as a medicine. Today, herbalists recommend anise to aid digestion and prevent gas. Because it loosens bronchial secretions and reduces coughing, anise is often found in cough syrups and lozenges. And the herb has some antimicrobial properties.

Anise is a prime ingredient in many cuisines, including Scandinavian, Greek, East Indian, Arabic, and Hispanic foods. The herb intensifies the flavor of pastries, cakes, and cookies, and it complements eggs, stewed fruit, cheese, spinach, and carrots. Use leaves whole in salads or as a garnish.

Name: <u>Arnica</u>

Botanical Name: *Arnica montana*

Description: Arnica, also called leopards-bane, mountain tobacco, and wolfsbane, is found in mountainous regions. The herb is indigenous to Europe and Siberia, but it has been naturalized in southwestern Canada and the western United States. Other species of arnica can be found from Alaska to New Mexico. The plant grows from a horizontal, dark brown root and produces round and hairy stems. These send up as many as three flower stalks with blossoms that resemble daisies and appear from June to August. Lance-shaped, bright green, and toothed, arnica's leaves appear somewhat hairy on their upper surfaces. The oval lower leaves grow to 5 inches long.

How to Plant: Arnica requires sandy, dry soil with humus and full sun. It prefers acidic soil but will grow in most beds as long as they are well drained. Some species of arnica tolerate light shade, including *A. cordifolia* and *A. latifolia*.

New arnica plants may be produced by means of division, cuttings, or seeds.

Uses: The next time your calves ache after a strenuous run, try massaging them with an arnica liniment. European herbalists and American Indians have long recognized arnica's abilities to soothe and relax sore, stiff muscles. More than 100 commercial preparations in Germany contain arnica. It is also used to make homeopathic remedies. The flower is the most potent part of the plant, but sometimes the leaves are also used.

Arnica's healing powers have been attributed to two chemicals, helenalin and arnicin, which have anti-inflammatory, antiseptic, and pain-relieving properties. Arnica also increases blood circulation.

Name: <u>Astragalus</u>

Botanical Name: *Astragalus membranaceus*

Description: Known as milk vetch in the West and huang qi in the East, this plant produces symmetrical oblong, pointed leaves. Astragalus is a member of the legume family, which includes lentils, beans, clover, and licorice.

How to Plant: Astragalus is not yet found in most herb gardens, but it is gaining popularity as its use in North America increases. In Asia, it is cultivated commercially or gathered in the wild.

Astragalus roots may be divided or grown from seed

Uses: Chinese physicians believe that astragalus is a tonic for the lung and spleen. Because of its immune-system-enhancing properties, astragalus is often prescribed for people with "wasting" diseases such as fatigue or loss of appetite due to chronic illness, or for people who need to strengthen their body's systems. It is also used to treat chronic diarrhea. It is not uncommon in China to use astragalus extracts to fight several kinds of cancer. It is used in Chinese hospitals to lessen the side effects of chemotherapy and radiation; studies have also found it improves survival rates of cancer patients.

Astragalus is an excellent diuretic. It lowers fevers and has a beneficial effect on the digestive system. Other illnesses for which herbalists use astragalus include arthritis; diabetes; inflammation in the urinary tract; prolapsed uterus, stomach, or anus; uterine bleeding and weakness; water retention; and skin wounds that refuse to heal.

Astragalus' ability to lower blood pressure is probably due to the gamma-aminobutyric acid it contains, which dilates blood vessels. Other chemicals in the root have been found to strengthen the lungs.

Name: Basil

Botanical Name: *Ocimum basilicum*

Description: Basil produces a neat, dense growth, with bright-green, triangular leaves. You can even clip basil into a neat hedge. Basil is native to India, Africa, and Asia and cultivated in France, Egypt, Hungary, Indonesia, Morocco, Greece, Bulgaria, the former Yugoslavian nations, and Italy. In the United States, it is widely grown in California and in kitchen gardens all over the country.

How to Plant: Basil prefers full sun and semi-rich, moist soil. It will grow in partial shade but gets "leggy" (it grows sparsely and doesn't fill out).

Sow seeds when soil is warm, or get a head start by planting seeds indoors and transplanting seedlings after the danger of frost is past.

Uses: A member of the mint family, basil is recommended to aid digestion and expel gas. It's also good for treating stomach cramps, vomiting, and constipation. It has been found to be more effective than drugs to relieve nausea from chemotherapy and radiation. Basil has a slight sedative action and sometimes is recommended for nervous headaches and anxiety. Extracts of basil seeds have anti-bacterial properties.

In the kitchen, basil's rich, spicy flavor—something like pepper with a hint of mint and cloves—works wonders in pesto, tomato sauce, salads, cheese dishes, eggs, stews, vinegars, and all sorts of vegetables.

Strongly fragrant, basil is used in sachets and potpourri. A basil infusion used as a hair rinse adds luster to the hair and helps treat acne and itching skin. Basil essential oil is found in perfumes and toilet waters, lotions, shampoos, and soaps. Added to the bath, it produces an invigorating soak.

Name: <u>Black Cohosh</u>

Botanical Name: *Cimicifuga racemosa*

Description: Related to buttercup, larkspur, and peony, black cohosh is a leafy herb with knotty black roots and a smooth stem. Also known as snakeroot, the plant produces small, multiple white flowers in midsummer on tall stalks. Black cohosh grows in the eastern United States and Canada.

How to Plant: Black cohosh is a wild plant that prefers rich soil and forest conditions. Seeds take two to four weeks to germinate and are best stratified.

Sow seed in spring; divide roots in spring or fall.

Uses: Native Americans used black cohosh to treat fatigue, sore throat, arthritis, and rattlesnake bite, but the herb's primary use historically was as a medicine to ease childbirth. Nineteenth-century American herbalists also recommended black cohosh for fever and menstrual cramps. Black cohosh is a diuretic, expectorant, astringent, and sedative, but today it is most often recommended for treating symptoms of menopause. The herb seems to have an estrogenic effect by binding to estrogen receptors in the body. Black cohosh contains salicylic acid (the main ingredient of aspirin) and has been used for a variety of muscular, pelvic, and rheumatic pains, especially those caused by nervous tension.

Name: <u>Blue Cohosh</u>

Botanical Name: *Caulophyllum thalictroides*

Description: Blue cohosh is a bluish-green, deciduous plant that flowers in June to August, producing yellow-green clusters of blooms on tall stalks. Blue cohosh is native to North America and grows from New Brunswick to Manitoba and south to Alabama. You may encounter blue cohosh in woods and along stream banks.

How to Plant: The herb likes rich, moist, humusy soil and shade.

Sow seeds in spring; if you plant them in fall, they may germinate the following spring. Divide rhizomes in spring or fall. Seeds and rhizomes are available through mail order from wild flower and herb sources.

Uses: Over the centuries and up to the present time, the herb has been used to treat uterine abnormalities and relieve menstrual cramps. Before the introduction of forceps, American obstetricians used blue cohosh to help induce labor.

In the past, blue cohosh was used to treat bronchitis, rheumatism, and irregular menstruation. It was also combined with other herbs, including motherwort and partridge berry, for women in the last few weeks of pregnancy to promote smooth labor.

Name: <u>Borage</u>

Botanical Name: *Borago officinalis*

Description: The herb's basal rosette of long, spear-shaped leaves produces tall stems covered with attractive, bright-blue, star-shaped flowers that hang downward. All parts of the plant are covered with bristly "hairs." Borage is a nice addition to any flower garden. Although usually grown as an annual, the plant will often overwinter in mild climates for a second growing season. Borage is native to Europe, Asia Minor, northern Europe, and Africa. It has become naturalized in Great Britain and is found widely in North America, often in waste places and along roads.

How to Plant: Borage prefers a dry, sunny location in poor to ordinary, well-drained soil. It is difficult to transplant; if you must do so, move the plant when it is young.

Sow seed in early spring or late fall.

Uses: Celtic warriors drank borage wine because they believed it gave them courage. Romans thought borage produced a sense of elation and well-being. The Greeks turned to the herb when their spirits sagged. Today, herbalists consider borage a diuretic, demulcent, and emollient, and prescribe the plant to treat depression, fevers, bronchitis, and diarrhea. The malic acid and potassium nitrate it contains may be responsible for its diuretic effects. Poultices of leaves may be useful in cooling and soothing skin and reducing inflammation and swelling. The plant also has expectorant properties.

The crisp flavor of borage flowers complements cheese, fish, poultry, most vegetables, salads, iced beverages, pickles, and salad dressings. You can eat small amounts of young leaves: Steam well as you would spinach so the leaves are no longer prickly. You can also candy the flowers.

Name: Burdock

Botanical Name: *Arctium lappa*

Description: This stout, coarse herb has many branches, each topped by numerous flowers, which appear in summer. The seed burrs cling to anything that rubs against them. The large leaves grow to 20 inches. Native to Eurasia, burdock has become naturalized throughout North America. You're likely to find burdock in fields and vacant lots, especially in damp areas.

How to Plant: A wild plant, burdock prefers average, moist, deep, loose, and well-drained soil and full sun, but it will grow in filtered sun.

Burdock is grown easily from seed sown in the spring. Seedlings transplant well, but older plants are more difficult to relocate because they produce long taproots.

Uses: If you've ever returned from an outdoor romp with your pet and discovered burrs clinging tenaciously to the cuffs of your trousers and your pet's fur, you've encountered burdock, an herb whose primary use is as a blood purifier. The root is also considered a diuretic, diaphoretic, and laxative. It has also been used to treat psoriasis, acne, and other skin conditions. Research has found that several compounds in burdock root inhibit growth of bacteria and fungi. A poultice of leaves is effective in healing bruises, burns, and swellings. The Chinese also use burdock root to treat colds, flu, measles, and constipation and burdock seeds to treat skin problems. Herbalists use burdock to treat liver disorders.

Burdock also contains a substance called inulin, a starch that is easily digested. Burdock root tastes like a marriage of potato and celery; eat it fresh or steamed. Eat young stalks raw or steam them as you would asparagus.

Name: <u>Burnet</u>

Botanical Name: *Poterium sanguisorba*

Description: A ground-hugging rosette of dark green leaves forms the plant, from which thin, 1 to 1 1/2-foot stems arise to produce handsome purple flower heads. Burnet makes a good edging plant. Also called salad burnet, the plant is native to western Asia and Europe and has become naturalized in North America.

How to Plant: Burnet prefers full sun in average soil, although rich soil improves its flavor, making it less bitter. Burnet prefers an alkaline soil; if your soil is very acidic, add lime.

Sow seed. Burnet self-sows easily after its first planting.

Uses: Herbalists have used burnet for at least 2,000 years. Useful to control bleeding, burnet's name, in fact, means "to drink up blood." Nineteenth-century Shakers used burnet for healing wounds. And the herb is considered helpful in treating vaginal discharges and diarrhea. Burnet leaves contain vitamin C and tannins; the latter gives it astringent properties. It relieves indigestion and diarrhea. Practitioners of traditional Chinese medicine use the root topically on wounds and burns to reduce inflammation and the risk of infection. It is also used to treat gum disease. While burnet is rarely used medicinally in North America, Europeans, and Russians still use it in their folk medicine. It is used to heal ulcerative colitis as a folk remedy in Northern Europe and Russia. The leaves also have immune-enhancing properties that may help correct some abnormalities during pregnancy.

In the kitchen, use tender, young, well-chopped leaves in salads, vinegars, butters, and iced beverages. Add leaves to vinegars, marinades, and cheese spreads. And flowers make attractive garnishes.

Name: <u>Butcher's Broom</u>

Botanical Name: *Ruscus aculeatus*

Description: For 300 years—from the 16th to 19th centuries—butcher's broom was associated with the meat industry. Butchers used the leaves to repel vermin and animals. Later, they made "brooms" from the plant to scrub chopping blocks. With its waxy green leaves and scarlet berries, butcher's broom has been used to decorate meats at Christmas; indeed, another name for the herb is box holly. Found naturally from the Azores to Iran, butcher's broom is an erect evergreen, with prickly leaves and whitish or pinkish flowers that appear from midautumn to late spring. Its round berries are scarlet or yellow. Butcher's broom is found in woodland thickets on poor, dry, soil.

How to Plant: Cultivate butcher's broom in regular garden soil. An attractive plant, it is available at many nurseries, sold as an ornamental.

Uses: Butcher's broom enjoys a venerable history as a medicinal herb. The ancient Greeks recommended butcher's broom for treating kidney stones, gout, and jaundice.

Butcher's broom has experienced a comeback in recent years. There is some evidence it may have value in treating circulatory problems, such as varicose veins and hemorrhoids. In German studies, it decreased the inflammation of varicose veins, helped to tighten them, and encouraged the blood to flow up the legs. In addition to strengthening blood vessels, the plant reduces fever and increases urine flow.

Name: <u>Calendula</u>

Botanical Name: *Calendula officinalis*

Description: Calendula produces coarse, bright green leaves attached to brittle stems. The plant grows rapidly and blooms abundantly throughout summer, until the first frost. Also called pot marigold, the herb's flower colors range from bright yellow to vivid orange. (It is not a true marigold.) Calendula is a cheerful addition to any garden and makes an attractive potted plant. Calendula is found naturally from the Canary Islands through southern and central Europe. It is cultivated widely around the world.

How to Plant: Calendula enjoys full sun and average, well-drained soil. Be on the lookout for insects, which adore calendula.

Sow seed outdoors in early spring or indoors about seven weeks before the last frost.

Uses: The herb is used today to treat wounds, skin conditions, and peptic and duodenal ulcers. Calendula's primary use is to heal the skin and reduce swelling. Apply calendula to sores, cuts, bruises, burns, and rashes. It even soothes the discomfort of measles and chicken pox—simply make a double strength tea and wash over the skin eruptions. It also helps prevent and relieve diaper rash. Calendula induces sweating, increases urination, and aids digestion. Researchers have found that compounds in calendula may be useful in treating cancer. It has traditionally been used to treat tonsillitis and any condition related to swollen lymph glands, including breast cancer.

In the kitchen, add a few calendula flowers to salads and sandwiches. Powdered yellow flowers may substitute for saffron's color (they once were used to color butter, custards, and liqueurs), although go easy—they have a bitter taste. The flowers produce a bright yellow dye and are commercially grown. Dry flowers for potpourri. A calendula rinse brings out highlights in hair. It is a popular ingredient in skin cream and lotions, baby oils, and salves.

Name: Caraway

Botanical Name: *Carum carvi*

Description: Although caraway is a biennial, some varieties behave as annuals, going to seed in their first year. Caraway is characterized by fine-cut leaves that resemble the foliage of carrots. White umbels develop in the plant's second year to produce distinctively flavored seeds. Native to the Middle East, Asia, and central Europe, caraway has become naturalized in North America.

How to Plant: Caraway grows best in a light, average, well-drained soil in full sun, although it tolerates partial shade. Plant in place; caraway produces a long taproot and does not transplant easily.

Sow seeds outdoors in early spring or late summer.

Uses: Caraway seeds were found in ancient tombs, indicating the plant was used at least 5,000 years ago. As a medicine, caraway is used—most often as a cordial—to relieve an upset stomach and dispel gas. Caraway water has long been given to babies with colic. A compress soaked in a strong infusion or the powdered and moistened seed relieves swelling and bruising. But you may be most familiar with caraway from eating sauerkraut, rye crackers, and rye bread—foods that rely heavily on its strong aroma and taste. Add caraway seeds to beef dishes stews, and breads. Add leaves to salads and soups. The herb complements eggs, cheese, sauces, barley, oats, pork, and fish, as well as cabbage, beets, spinach, potatoes, peas, cauliflower, turnips, and zucchini. Cooking it a long time can make it bitter, so add caraway no more than 30 minutes before a dish is done. It also makes children's medicines tastier. The essential oil is added to soaps, cosmetics, perfumes, and mouthwashes and used to flavor liqueurs in Germany, Scandinavia, and Russia.

Name: Catnip

Botanical Name: *Nepeta cataria*

Description: Also called catmint, this herb produces fuzzy, gray-green, triangular leaves in pairs along abundant branches. The leaves give off a pungent scent when crushed. From July through September, catnip produces white flowers with purple or pink spots. The herb is native to the Eurasian region and naturalized throughout North America and elsewhere.

How to Plant: Catnip grows well in full sun to partial shade, in average to sandy, well-drained soil.

Sow seed in spring or fall; take cuttings in early summer.

Uses: Your cat may go crazy over catnip, but the herb has actually been used as a mild sedative for about 2,000 years. The Romans harvested catnip, and colonists carried the herb to America, where it quickly became naturalized. Catnip tea aids digestion, promotes sleep, and treats colds, nervousness, and headaches. Its most important use is as a sedative that is safe enough even for children and the elderly. Catnip contains sedative constituents similar to valerian, another popular herbal relaxant. One of catnip's most famous uses is to treat colic in babies—a condition for which it has been used for hundreds of years. It also makes a good tea for treating indigestion associated with anxiety or nervousness. The tea treats measles and chicken pox when used both internally and topically. An infusion applied to the skin relieves hives and other rashes. The herb increases perspiration, reduces fevers, and increases menstrual flow. The herb's fragrance also repels some insects.

Catnip is usually combined with other herbs in a tea or tincture. For indigestion or for use as a gentle sedative, mix it with chamomile and lemon balm.

Name: <u>Cayenne Pepper</u>

Botanical Name: *Capsicum annuum*

Description: Cayenne's angular branches and stems may look purplish. Its red fruits are extremely hot. Flowers, which appear in drooping clusters on long stems, are star-shaped and yellowish-white. Leaves are long and elliptical. Cayenne grows naturally in the tropics, but gardeners in most parts of the United States can grow it with success.

How to Plant: Unless you live in an area that rarely experiences freezing temperatures, it's best to plant cayenne in containers you can bring inside when temperatures drop, or grow it as an annual. The plant grows best in rich soil. If your soil is average, fertilize it with compost, rock phosphate, or wood ashes. Cayenne likes full sun. Give your plants lots of water during early stages of growth.

Because cayenne has a long growing season (up to 18 weeks), start plants indoors if propagating from seed. Transplant seedlings 12 to 18 inches apart, and allow 3 feet between rows.

Uses: Cayenne has many medicinal uses. The main ingredient in cayenne is capsaicin, a powerful stimulant responsible for the pepper's heat. Although it can set your mouth on fire, cayenne, ironically, is good for your digestive system and is now known to help heal ulcers. It reduces substance P, a chemical that carries pain messages from the skin's nerve endings, so it reduces pain when applied topically. A cayenne cream is now in use to treat psoriasis, postsurgical pain, shingles, and nerve damage from diabetes.

Taking cayenne internally stabilizes blood pressure. You can apply powdered, dry cayenne as a poultice over wounds to stop bleeding. And in the kitchen, cayenne spices up any food it touches.

Name: <u>Chamomile</u>

Botanical Name: *Matricaria recutita*

Description: These small, fine-leaved plants look almost like ferns, but the herb's abundant, small, daisy-type flowers have an apple scent. German chamomile looks much like its cousin, Roman chamomile (*Chamaemelum nobile*), but German chamomile is an annual and must be grown from seed each spring. Roman chamomile may spread to form a lush mat, which can be mowed regularly. Both chamomile species are native to Europe, Africa, and Asia and have become naturalized in North America. Chamomile is widely cultivated. There are other species of chamomile, including several that are indigenous to North America.

How to Plant: Chamomile grows in full sun, in average to poor, light, dry soil. Plant several chamomiles; single plants are too small to have any impact in a garden.

Sow seed in early spring; divide in the spring or fall.

Uses: Chamomile is one of the world's best-loved herbs. The herb produces a pleasant-tasting tea, which has a strong aroma of apples. The early Egyptians valued chamomile and used it to cure malaria and bring down fevers. The ancient Greeks called on chamomile to relieve headaches and treat illnesses of the kidney, liver, and bladder. Today herbalists prescribe the herb to calm nerves and settle upset stomachs, among its other uses.

Chamomile's medicinal properties derive from its essential oils. The herb has three primary medicinal uses: an anti-inflammatory to reduce swelling and infection; an antispasmodic to relieve digestive upsets, headaches, and menstrual cramps; and an anti-infective for cleansing wounds.

Drink as much chamomile tea as you wish. Use up to 1 and 1/2 teaspoons (6 droppers full) of tincture a day. You can also take chamomile as pills, or use it in a vinegar or skin cream. Use a chamomile compress, poultice, or tincture on bruises and inflammation.

Chamomile flowers may cause symptoms of allergies in some people allergic to ragweed and related plants, although the risk of this is quite low.

147

Name: <u>Chaste Tree</u>

Botanical Name: *Vitex agnus castus*

Description: Chaste tree is a small tree, with opposite leaves divided into lanceolate leaflets. Its small flowers are lavender or lilac. Native to southern Europe, the herb has been naturalized in warm regions.

How to Plant: Chaste tree likes sandy or loamy, well-drained soil and full sun.

Sow seed in spring; layer or take young woody cuttings in spring.

Uses: Chaste tree, which is often referred to as Vitex, is used primarily to treat women's discomforts. The flavonoids in chaste tree produce a progesterone-like effect. The herb may raise progesterone levels by acting on the brain. Chaste tree helps to normalize and regulate menstrual cycles, reduce premenstrual fluid retention, reduce some cases of acne that may flare up during PMS or menstruation, reduce hot flashes, and treat menopausal bleeding irregularities and other menopausal symptoms. It is also useful in helping dissolve fibroids and cysts in the reproductive system and may be used for treating some types of infertility.

Chaste tree has been used after childbirth to promote milk production. It is a slow-acting herb and may take months to take effect. Because of its complex hormonal actions, be cautious using chaste tree during pregnancy. It may also interfere with hormonal drugs.

Name: <u>Chives</u>

Botanical Name: *Allium schoenoprasum*

Description: Chives produces clumps of thin leaves that resemble those of onion in appearance and taste. The herb produces abundant, small, rose-purple, globe-shaped flower heads in early summer. Chives may be grown alone or with other plants in containers. The herb is native to Greece, Sweden, the Alps, and parts of northern Great Britain.

How to Plant: Chives prefers an average to rich soil but manages in almost any soil. The herb grows best in full sun to partial shade. Chives makes a good ornamental plant in the garden. Chives may also be grown as a potted plant indoors at any time of the year. Several new varieties have been developed to produce thicker bunches and longer-lasting flowers. Chives is said to complement growth of carrots, grapes, roses, and tomatoes.

Sow seed or divide at any time during the growing season.

Uses: Archaeologists tell us that chives have been in use for at least 5,000 years. By the 16th century, it was a popular European garden herb. Chives' few medicinal properties derive from the sulfur-rich oil found in all members of the onion family. The oil is antiseptic and may help lower blood pressure, but it must be consumed in fairly large quantities. Chives' pleasant taste—like that of mild, sweet onions—complements the flavor of most foods. Use fresh minced leaves in dishes containing potatoes, artichokes, asparagus, cauliflower, corn, tomatoes, peas, carrots, spinach, poultry, fish, veal, cheese, eggs, and, of course, in cream cheese atop your bagel or in sour cream on a baked potato. Add chives at the last minute for best flavor. Flowers are good additions to salads and may be preserved in vinegars.

Name: <u>Comfrey</u>

Botanical Name: *Symphytum officinale*

Description: Comfrey is a hardy, leafy plant that dies down in winter and comes back strong in spring. The herb produces roots that are black outside and white in-side and exude a mucilaginous substance when crushed. Various species of comfrey have purple-pink flowers and appear from May through the first frost. The herb is native to Europe and Asia and has become naturalized on every continent. Comfrey is found along stream banks and in moist meadows.

How to Plant: Comfrey prefers rich to average soil and full sun or partial shade but will grow almost anywhere. The herb is easy to grow, but it is very invasive and difficult to eradicate, so plant it where you can contain it. Once established, comfrey requires little maintenance, but you will have it there forever!

Sow seed in spring, divide in fall, take cuttings any time. Set plants 3 feet apart.

Uses: Comfrey has been regarded as a great healer since at least around 400 B.C., when the Greeks used it topically to stop bleeding, heal wounds, and mend broken bones. The Romans made comfrey poultices and teas to treat bruises, stomach disorders, and diarrhea. Today herbalists continue to prescribe comfrey for bruises, wounds, and sores. Allantoin, a compound found in comfrey, causes cells to divide and grow, spurring wounds to heal faster. It also inhibits inflammation of the stomach's lining. Comfrey has been recommended for treating bronchitis, asthma, respiratory irritation, peptic ulcers, and stomach and intestinal inflammation. Studies show it inhibits pros-taglandins, substances that cause inflammation. It was once promoted as a salad green and potherb; however, internal use of comfrey has become a much-debated topic.

In cosmetic use, comfrey soothes and softens skin and promotes growth of new cells. Comfrey is found in creams, lotions, and bath preparations. It dyes wool brown.

Name: <u>Coriander</u>

Botanical Name: *Coriandrum sativum*

Description: Coriander's bright green, lacy leaves resemble those of flat-leaved Italian parsley when they first spring up from seed, but they become more fernlike as the plant matures. Coriander, also called cilantro and Chinese parsley, flowers from middle to late summer. The herb is native to the eastern Mediterranean region and southern Europe.

How to Plant: Coriander prefers average, well-drained soil in full sun. Protect fragile stalks from wind. Coriander may enhance growth of anise.

Sow seed in spring after soil is warm.

Uses: Coriander has been cultivated for 3,000 years. The Hebrews, who used coriander seed as one of their Passover herbs, probably learned about it from the ancient Egyptians, who revered the plant. The Romans and Greeks used coriander for medicinal purposes and as a spice and preservative. Throughout northern Europe, people would suck on candy-coated coriander seeds when they had indigestion; chewing the seeds soothes an upset stomach, relieves flatulence, aids digestion, and improves appetite. But its most popular medicinal use has been to flavor strong-tasting medicines and to prevent intestinal gripping common with some laxative formulas.

Add young leaves to beets, onions, salads, sausage, clams, oysters, and potatoes. Add seeds to marinades, salad dressings, cheese, eggs, and pickling brines. Its essential oil is found in perfumes, aftershaves, and cosmetics because of its delightfully spicy scent.

Name: <u>Costmary</u>

Botanical Name: *Chrysanthemum balsamita*

Description: Costmary produces basal clusters of elongated oval leaves. The herb sends up tall flower stems that produce clusters of unremarkable blooms. When leaves are young and fresh, they smell spicy; the scent changes to balsam when the leaves are dried. The herb is native to western Asia. Although it's rarely found growing in the wild, it is cultivated throughout Europe and North America.

How to Plant: Costmary prefers fertile, well-drained soil in full sun to partial shade.

Divide as needed and every few years as clumps become large.

Uses: Costmary flourished in English gardens and was used to spice ale. The herb is antiseptic and slightly astringent and has been used in salves to heal dry, itchy skin. It promotes urine flow and brings down fevers. Although rarely used for this purpose today, its principle medicinal use was as a digestive aid and to treat dysentery, for which it was included in the *British Pharmacopoeia*. The cosmetic water was commonly used to improve the complexion and as a hair rinse. Costmary is good for acne and oily skin and hair.

Costmary's flavor complements beverages, chilled soups, and fruit salads. You can add dried leaves to potpourri, sachets, and baths, or slip them in books to deter bugs that eat paper—this was once a common practice. Dried branches have been used to make herbal baskets.

Costmary is rarely used medicinally, but you could make a tea of the leaves. However, the tea tastes bitter, so add sweeter herbs such as lemon balm and mint.

Name: <u>Cramp Bark</u>

Botanical Name: *Viburnum opulus*

Description: A relative of black haw and sloe, cramp bark was introduced to England in the 16th century from Holland, where it is known as guelder rose. Also called highbush cranberry or snowball tree, cramp bark has multiple branches that produce three to five lobed, shiny leaves. White flowers appear from early to middle summer, followed by scarlet berries that eventually turn purple. The tree is native to Europe, North Africa, and northern Asia and has become naturalized elsewhere, particularly in Canada and the northern United States.

How to Plant: Cramp bark likes moist, average to rich soil and full sun.

Cramp bark grows from seed, although seeds need stratification and may take months to germinate. New shrubs also grow from hardwood cuttings. The easiest way to obtain the herb is to buy a plant from the nursery—it is a popular landscape plant.

Uses: Cramp bark's name tells you how the tree is used. American Indian women relied extensively on cramp bark to ease the pain of menstrual cramps and childbirth. An early American formula known as Mother's Cordial was given to women in childbirth. Cramp bark is used to halt contractions during premature labor and prevent miscarriage. It has also been used to prevent uterine hemorrhaging.

An antispasmodic, cramp bark may reduce leg cramps, muscle spasms, and pain from a stiff neck. Nineteenth-century herbalists often prescribed cramp bark as a sedative and muscle relaxant. The herb's medicinal actions may be attributed in part to a bitter called viburnin, as well as valerianic acid (also found in valerian), salicosides (also found in willow bark), and an antispasmodic constituent. Clinical studies indicate cramp bark may be useful in treating cardiovascular problems, reducing blood pressure and heart palpitations, and fighting influenza viruses. Cramp bark is considered an astringent as well.

Name: <u>Dill</u>

Botanical Name: *Anethum graveolens*

Description: Dill produces fine-cut, fernlike leaves on tall, fragile stems. It is a blue-green annual with attractive yellow flower umbels and yellow-green seed heads. The herb blooms from July through September. Native to the Mediterranean region and southwest Asia, it has become naturalized throughout North America.

How to Plant: Dill likes light, moist, sandy soil in full sun. Because it does not transplant well, sow in place and thin as needed. Grow dill in clumps or rows, so fragile stems can support each other. Some gardeners believe dill enhances the growth of cabbage, onions, and lettuce.

Sow seed in late fall or early spring. Plant at three-week intervals during spring and early summer for a fresh supply all season.

Uses: Dill derives from an old Norse word meaning "to lull," and, indeed, the herb once was used to induce sleep in babies with colic. Herbalists also use dill to relieve gas and to stimulate flow of mother's milk. Dill stimulates the appetite and settles the stomach, but the seeds have also been chewed to lessen the appetite and stop the stomach from rumbling—something that parishioners found useful during all-day church services.

Add minced dill leaves to salads and use as a garnish. Seeds go well with fish, lamb, pork, poultry, cheese, cream, eggs, and an array of vegetables, including cabbage, onions, cauliflower, squash, spinach, potatoes, and broccoli. Of course, dill pickles would not be the same without dill seed and weed.

Name: Echinacea

Botanical Name: *Echinacea purpurea*

Description: Also known as purple coneflower, echinacea resembles the black-eyed Susan. The herb produces long black roots and stout, sturdy stems covered with bristly hairs. Cone-shaped flower heads, which appear from middle to late summer, are composed of numerous tiny purple florets surrounded by deep pink petals. Leaves are pale green to dark green. Echinacea is native to prairies from southern Canada to Texas.

How to Plant: Echinacea prefers average, well-drained soil and full sun to light shade. The herb may fall prey to leaf spot or Japanese beetles.

Sow seed in spring. Mulch in winter. Dig up the plant about every four years, divide, and replant in fertilized soil.

Uses: American Indians used echinacea extensively to treat the bites of snakes and poisonous insects, burns, and wounds; the root facilitates wound healing. (Sometimes the seeds are combined with the roots for medicinal use.) Echinacea is prescribed to treat various infections, mumps, measles, and eczema. A compound in echinacea prevents damage to collagen in the skin and connective tissues when taken internally. Recent studies suggest that, applied topically, echinacea may treat sunburn.

Today, echinacea root is used primarily to boost the immune system and help the body fight disease. Besides bolstering several chemical substances that direct immune response, echinacea increases the number and activity of white blood cells (the body's disease-fighting agents), raises the level of interferon (a substance that enhances immune function), increases production of substances the body produces to fight cancers, and helps remove pollutants from the lungs. Many studies support echinacea's ability to fend off disease.

Name: <u>Elderberry</u>

Botanical Name: *Sambucus nigra*

Description: Elderberry comprises about 13 species of deciduous shrubs native to North America and Europe. European settlers brought elderberry plants with them to the American colonies. Its flowers are white and plate-shaped, the leaves are pinnate (resembling a feather) and may be toothed, and its fruit appears in purple-blue clusters.

How to Plant: Elderberry prefers fertile, moist soil and full sun to partial shade. Propagate the suckers or grow plants from seeds or cuttings. Elderberry may require maintenance since it likes to sprawl.

Uses: Elderberry has probably been used medicinally for as long as human beings have gathered plants. Evidence of elderberry plants has been uncovered in Stone Age sites. Ancient people used elderberries to dye their hair black. The wood of old stems is still used to make musical instruments by Native Americans and Europeans.

In the kitchen, the berries are used to make jams, jellies, chutneys, preserves, wines, and teas. For decades, elder flower water was on the dressing tables of proper young ladies who used it to treat sunburn and eradicate freckles. It is still sometimes used in Europe for these purposes. Yellow and violet dyes are made from the leaves and berries, respectively.

Medicinally, elderberry has been used as a mild digestive stimulant and diaphoretic. Elder flowers decrease inflammation, so they are often included in preparations to treat burns and swellings and in cosmetics that reduce puffiness. The berries have been used traditionally in Europe to treat flu, gout, and rheumatism as well as to improve general health. Several tales attribute longevity to the elderberry.

Name: <u>Evening Primrose</u>

Botanical Name: *Oenothera biennis*

Description: Some people are so busy during the day they don't have time to enjoy their herb gardens until after the moon rises. If you're one of those folks, evening primrose is the perfect herb for your garden. Its clear yellow flowers unclasp and blossom in the evening. Later in the growing season, evening primrose flowers may remain open during the day. Evening primrose flowers from early summer to mid-autumn. The stem is sturdy, rough, hairy, and reddish; its seeds round, beige, and oily.

How to Plant: Don't try to grow evening primrose indoors. The plant needs a sunny, open site, with well-drained soil.

Sow seeds in spring to early summer; thin to 12 inches by autumn.

Uses: The boiled root of evening primrose, which tastes something like a sweet parsnip, may be pickled or tossed raw in salads. The plant once was grown in monasteries; more recently scientists have found that the seeds contain a rare substance called gamma-Linolenic acid (better known as GLA), which may have value in treating multiple sclerosis, thrombosis, premenstrual symptoms, menopausal discomfort, alcohol withdrawal, hyperactivity, and psoriasis. In one study, more than half the study participants found that their PMS symptoms completely disappeared when they used evening primrose. In another study, more than half the arthritis patients who took evening primrose oil also found relief. The oil, when combined with zinc supplements, improves dry eyes and brittle nails, although it often takes two to three months to notice improvement in these conditions. Leaves and bark have been used to ease cough spasms.

Evening primrose also helps regenerate damaged liver cells. It is thought to prevent liver damage, stop alcohol from impairing brain cells, and lessen the symptoms of a hangover.

Name: <u>Fennel</u>

Botanical Name: *Foeniculum vulgare*

Description: With its feathery leaves, fennel looks much like a large version of its relative, dill. This fairly hardy perennial flowers from June through October. Sweet fennel (*F. vulgare dulce*), the variety sold in grocery stores, produces celery-like stalks known as finochhio. Both varieties taste similar to anise or licorice. Fennel is native to the Mediterranean region and widely naturalized elsewhere. It loves to grow by the ocean and near streams.

How to Plant: Fennel likes alkaline soil; you can add lime if soil is very acidic, although the herb is not fussy. Grow in full sun to partial shade in well-drained, average soil. Shelter fennel from heavy winds because the plant's fragile stems blow over easily.

Sow seeds in late fall or early spring.

Uses: The Greeks gave fennel to nursing mothers to increase milk flow. Early physicians also considered fennel a remedy for poor eyesight, weight loss, hiccups, nausea, gout, and many other illnesses. Fennel is a carminative (relieves gas and pain in the bowels), weak diuretic, and mild digestive stimulant. Herbalists often recommend fennel tea to soothe an upset stomach and dispel gas. It aids digestion, especially of fat.

Fennel tastes like a more bitter version of anise. Use leaves in salads and as garnishes. You can eat tender stems as you would celery, and add seeds to desserts, breads, cakes, cookies, and beverages. Mince bulbs of sweet fennel and eat raw or braise. Fennel complements fish, sausage, duck, barley, rice, cabbage, beets, pickles, potatoes, lentils, breads, and eggs. Add it to butters, cheese spreads, and salad dressings.

Name: <u>Feverfew</u>

Botanical Name: *Tanacetum parthenium*

Description: Feverfew is an erect herb that produces a branched root and many stems. Its multiple flowers are small and white, with yellow centers, like its cousin, the daisy, and it looks somewhat like chamomile. Flowers appear from midsummer through fall. Feverfew's leaves are yellowish green with a bitter scent. The herb is native to central and southern Europe and has become naturalized throughout temperate regions, including North and South America.

How to Plant: Feverfew prefers average, well-drained soil and full sun to partial shade.

Sow seeds or divide roots in spring. Take cuttings in fall or spring.

Uses: Feverfew's common name derives from the Latin *febrifugia*, which means "driver out of fevers." The Romans used the herb extensively for this purpose, and the Greeks employed it to normalize irregular contractions in childbirth. Today feverfew leaves are best known for their ability to fight headaches, particularly migraines. The herb's constituents relax blood vessels in the brain and inhibit secretion of substances that cause pain. Feverfew is most effective when used long-term to prevent chronic migraines, but some people find it helpful when taken at the onset of a headache. When patients at the Department of Medicine and Haemotology in Nottingham, England, ate fresh feverfew leaves for three months, they had fewer migraines and less nausea when they did experience one. Their blood pressure was reduced, and they reported feelings of well-being. Feverfew also is reported to reduce inflammation in joints and tissues. It has been prescribed for treating menstrual cramps.

Pyrethrin, an active ingredient, is a potent insect repellent. Feverfew's leaves and stems produce a dye that is greenish-yellow.

Name: <u>Garlic</u>

Botanical Name: *Allium sativum*

Description: Garlic produces a compound bulb composed of numerous cloves encased in a papery sheath. Flowers are small and white to pinkish. Long, slender green leaves arise from the bulb. The herb may have originated in southern Siberia; it is cultivated extensively around the world.

How to Plant: Garlic likes rich, deep, well-drained soil and full sun. Garlic contains fungicides and is thought to repel pests from companion plants.

Sow seeds in the fall or plant cloves in early spring for a midsummer harvest. Plant cloves with the pointed side up.

Uses: Garlic has been prized for millennia, used by the Egyptians, Hebrews, Romans, Greeks, and Chinese. Garlic is one of the most extensively researched and widely used plants. Its actions are diverse and affect nearly every body system. The herb boasts antibiotic, antifungal, and antiviral properties and is reported to be effective against many influenza strains.

Garlic's strong oniony taste has endeared it to cooks all over the world. You may add garlic to butters, cheese spreads, breads, all sorts of vegetables, stuffings, sauces, marinades, salad dressings, stews, soups, and meat dishes. Dried flower heads make an interesting addition to floral arrangements.

Name: <u>Gentian</u>

Botanical Name: *Gentiana lutea*

Description: Also called bitter root, gentian produces an interesting-looking root that may grow 1 to 2 feet long and 1 to 2 inches thick. Fresh roots are pale yellow; roots have a strong, perhaps disagreeable odor and are extremely bitter. Gentian's leaves, found at each stem joint, are smooth, waxy, and oval and light to medium green.

How to Plant: Gentian likes neutral to acid soil that is moist and well drained. The plant requires partial shade. Once satisfactorily transplanted, the plants require little attention. But they need abundant moisture and shelter from cold, dry winds and direct sunshine. Once a year, refresh the bed with acid soil or peat moss. If the temperature in your area dips well below freezing, mulch gentian with hay or evergreen boughs to protect it.

It's possible, though difficult, to grow gentian from seeds, which require frost or stratification to germinate. Even then, they may take up to a year to produce seedlings. For most gardeners, the best bet is to start gentian plants from crown divisions or transplanted roots.

Uses: Gentian root has been prized as a digestive bitter for more than 3,000 years—the Egyptians, Arabs, Greeks, and Romans used it. In India, Ayurvedic doctors used gentian to treat fevers, venereal disease, jaundice, and other illnesses of the liver. Colonists in Virginia and the Carolinas discovered Native Americans using a gentian decoction to treat back pain. Chinese physicians use it to treat digestive disorders, sore throat, headache, and arthritis. Gentian, moreover, has been used to increase menstruation, thus easing painful periods.

Today, gentian is used commercially to make liqueurs, vermouth, digestive bitters, and aperitifs. The herb's bitterness increases gastric secretions and helps a sluggish appetite or poor digestion. It is especially useful for problems digesting fat or protein. Researchers in Germany found that it cures heartburn, intestinal inflammation, and general indigestion. It also destroys several types of intestinal worms.

Name: <u>Geranium</u>

Botanical Name: *Pelargonium graveolens*

Description: Botanically, these fragrant plants are not really geraniums, but pelargoniums. The leaves are frilly, soft, and well-veined; if you rub against them they emit a distinctive fragrance. The flowers are pink and unscented. The leaves of the different species come in a variety of shapes and sizes. Native to South Africa, the scented geranium has become naturalized in the eastern Mediterranean region, India, Australia, and New Zealand.

How to Plant: A tender plant, the scented geranium will not tolerate freezing temperatures. It needs rich, dry, loamy, well-drained soil and light shade.

The plants are best started from cuttings in spring or summer and transplanted after two to three weeks.

Uses: You could call the scented geranium the potpourri plant. The herb comes in a wide variety of fragrances, including rose, apple, lemon, lime, apricot, strawberry, coconut, and peppermint, making it an ideal addition to potpourri and sachets. The plant was considered fashionable in Colonial and Victorian times.

Herbalists sometimes recommend the astringent herb for treating diarrhea and ulcers and to stop bleeding. The essential oil is used to treat ringworm, lice, shingles, and herpes. The pharmaceutical industry uses one of the antiseptic compounds in geranium called geraniol. The leaves of some varieties, including rose, may be used to flavor cookies and jelly. Add other leaves, such as peppermint, to herbal teas. Added to facial steams and baths, they are cleansing and healing to the skin. The scent is popular in men's products—it blends well with woodsy and citrus fragrances. Rose geranium is used in many aromatherapy products for its relaxing and emotional balancing properties. This species is also added to cosmetics to improve the complexion.

Name: <u>Ginger</u>

Botanical Name: *Zingiber officinale*

Description: This tropical, aromatic herb produces a knotty, buff-colored tuberous rhizome. Leaves are grasslike, and flowers are dense, conelike, greenish-purple spikes with edging. Native to southeast Asia, ginger is cultivated elsewhere, including south Florida.

How to Plant: Ginger requires fertile, moist, well-drained soil and full sun to partial shade. The plant thrives in hot, humid climates, making it suitable for gardens in parts of the American South. Elsewhere, grow ginger in a greenhouse or indoors in a container.

Purchase green roots from a nursery or grocery store and plant the "eyes" in loam, sand, peat moss, and compost.

Uses: Most every child knows the taste of ginger. It's the prime ingredient in ginger ale, gingerbread, and gingersnaps. It's also a potent anti-nausea medication, useful for treating morning sickness, motion sickness, and nausea accompanying gastroenteritis (stomach "flu").

Ginger is a staple of many cuisines, including those of southeast Asia, India, Japan, the Caribbean, and North Africa. Add the spicy chopped root to beverages, fruits, meats, fish, preserves, pickles, and a variety of vegetables. Use ground ginger in breads, cookies, and other desserts.

Name: <u>Ginkgo</u>

Botanical Name: *Ginkgo biloba*

Description: This stately deciduous tree produces male and female flowers on separate plants. Female plants produce orange-yellow fruits the size of large olives. In the fall its leaves turn gold. Found throughout the temperate world, ginkgo may be grown in the United States.

How to Plant: Ginkgo requires well-drained soil. The trees are largely resistant to insects, drought, and diseases.

Plant saplings in spring.

Uses: Ginkgo is one of the oldest species of tree on earth. It is used to treat conditions associated with aging, including stroke, heart disease, impotence, deafness, ringing in the ears, blindness, and memory loss. In many studies, it helped people improve their concentration and memory. Ginkgo promotes the action of certain neurotransmitters, chemical compounds responsible for relaying nerve impulses in the brain.

Ginkgo increases circulation, including blood flow to the brain, which may help improve memory. Several studies show it reduces the risk of heart attack and improves pain from blood clots (phlebitis) in the legs. Additional studies show that, in a large percentage of people, ginkgo helps impotence caused by narrowing of arteries that supply blood to the penis; macular degeneration of the eyes, a deterioration in vision that may be caused by narrowing of the blood vessels to the eye; and cochlear deafness, which is caused by decreased blood flow to the nerves involved in hearing.

Name: Ginseng, American

Botanical Name: *Panax quinquefolius*

Description: American ginseng produces a single stem, a whorl of leaves, and several green-white flowers from June through August. Leaves are toothed; the berries, bright red. American ginseng is indigenous to Manitoba and Quebec and ranges south to Georgia and west through Alabama to Oklahoma.

How to Plant: Ginseng needs to be pampered but can be grown in home gardens. The herb demands shade and, rich, well-drained loam. Commercially, ginseng is grown in shelters that mimic forests. The plant must be mulched in winter and takes from five to seven years to produce usable roots, which often fall prey to rotting diseases or gophers.

Ginseng seeds require a cold period of at least four months to germinate. The most common way to grow it is to buy seedlings two to three years old.

Uses: The Chinese have used a close relative of American ginseng since prehistoric times. In the United States, colonists grew rich collecting American ginseng and ex-porting it to China, where the herb enjoys a strong reputation as an aphrodisiac and prolonger of life. Ginseng is an adaptogen, capable of protecting the body from physical and mental stress and helping bodily functions return to normal.

Clinical studies indicate that ginseng may slow the effects of aging, protect cells from free radical damage, prevent heart disease, and help treat anemia, atherosclerosis, de-pression, diabetes, edema (excess fluid buildup), ulcers, and hypertension. Its complex saponins, ginsenosides, are responsible for most of its actions. They stimulate bone marrow production and immune-system functions, inhibit tumor growth, and detoxify the liver. Ginseng has many dual roles, for example, raising or lowering blood pressure or blood sugar, according to the body's needs.

Ginseng gently stimulates and strengthens the central nervous system, making it useful for treating fatigue and weakness caused by disease and injury.

Name: <u>Goldenseal</u>

Botanical Name: *Hydrastis canadensis*

Description: Goldenseal is small and erect, with hairy stems growing from a twisted, knotted rhizome that is brown on the outside and bright yellow on the inside. The herb's solitary flowers are white and appear usually in May or June. One or two maple-leaf- shaped leaves appear at the base of the plant. Berries are orange-red and contain two shiny black seeds. Native to North America, the herb is found in moist, rich woodlands, damp meadows, and forest highlands.

How to Plant: Overharvesting of wild plants has put goldenseal on the endangered list. (You can use Oregon grape root as an alternative to goldenseal. It also contains golden-seal's active ingredient, berberine, and is much less expensive.)

Sow seeds in fall or stratify them. New plants also grow from root division.

Uses: The Cherokee tribe mixed powdered goldenseal root with bear grease and slathered their bodies to protect themselves from mosquitoes and other insects. Pioneers adopted the herb and used it to treat wounds, rashes, mouth sores, morning sickness, liver and stomach complaints, internal hemorrhaging, depressed appetite, constipation, and urinary and uterine problems.

One of goldenseal's active ingredients is hydrastine, which affects circulation, muscle tone, and uterine contractions. The herb is also an antiseptic, astringent, and antibiotic, making it effective for treating eye and other types of infections. Berberine and related alkaloids have been credited with goldenseal's antimicrobial effects. Goldenseal makes a good antiseptic skin wash for wounds and for internal skin surfaces, such as in the vagina and ear; it also treats canker sores and infected gums.

Name: <u>Hawthorn</u>

Botanical Name: *Crataegus laevigata*

Description: Like many members of the rose family, hawthorn bears thorns as well as lovely, fragrant flowers and brightly pigmented berries high in vitamin C. As many as 900 species of hawthorn exist in North America, ranging from deciduous trees to thorny-branched shrubs. Hawthorn produces white flower clusters in May. The herb is native to Europe, with closely related species in North Africa and western Asia.

How to Plant: Hawthorn tolerates a wide variety of soils but prefers ground that is alkaline, rich, loamy, and moist. Hawthorn also likes full sun. The tree sometimes falls prey to aphids and other insects and fungus.

Sow seed in the spring. Certain varieties of hawthorn must be grafted or budded. Smaller trees transplant better than larger ones. Trees are sold in most nurseries.

Uses: Hawthorn has been cherished for centuries. The Druids considered hawthorn a sacred tree. The Pilgrims brought it to America: Mayflower is, in fact, another name for hawthorn.

Hawthorn is an important herb for treating heart conditions. The berries and flowers contain several complex chemical constituents, including flavonoids such as anthocyanidins, which improve the strength of capillaries and reduce damage to blood vessels from oxidizing agents. Hawthorn's ability to dilate blood vessels, enhancing circulation, makes it useful for treating angina, atherosclerosis, high and low blood pressure, and elevated cholesterol levels. Many clinical studies have demonstrated its effectiveness for such conditions—with the use of hawthorn, the heart requires less oxygen when under stress. Heart action is normalized and becomes stronger and more efficient. Hawthorn also helps balance the heart's rhythm and is prescribed for arrhythmias and heart palpitations by European physicians. Although it affects the heart somewhat like the medication digitalis, hawthorn does not have a cumulative effect on the heart.

Name: Hops

Botanical Name: *Humulus lupulus*

Description: Like the grape, hops is a quick-growing and quick-spreading vine. Each year a stem grows from the root and begins to twine. After the third year, hops produce a papery, conelike fruit called a strobile. Male and female flowers grow on separate plants and appear from middle to late summer. Hops leaves somewhat resemble grape leaves, hairy and coarse, with serrated edges. A relative of marijuana, hops is native to Europe and can be found in vacant fields and along rivers. Most hops grown in the United States is for the beer industry, which uses hops to flavor its products.

How to Plant: Hops can be grown as a garden plant. Vines also are grown commercially in hopyards on wires strung between poles. Hops requires full sun, deep, well-drained soil, and good air circulation to prevent mildew from forming.

Hops may be started from cuttings or suckers taken in early summer from healthy old plants.

Uses: If you worked in a hopyard, you might find yourself falling asleep on the job. Hops contains chemicals that depress the central nervous system, making it a useful sedative herb. Both Abraham Lincoln and England's King George III, notorious insomniacs, reportedly lay their heads on hops-filled pillows to ensure a good night's sleep. Hops' other constituents are antiseptic, antibacterial, and anti-inflammatory, and they slightly increase activity of the female hormone estrogen. Hops has also been used as a pain reliever, fever cure, expectorant, and diuretic.

Drink hops tea up to three times a day. Take 1/2 to 1 teaspoon (2 to 4 droppers full) of tincture up to three times a day or take it in pills. Hops is often mixed with other sedative herbs or herbs that help relieve menstrual or menopausal symptoms.

Name: <u>Horehound</u>

Botanical Name: *Marrubium vulgare*

Description: A member of the mint family, horehound has branching stems, which may give it a bushy appearance. Leaves have a "woolly" look, and flowers appear in dense white whorls in summer. Horehound is native to southern Europe, central and western Asia, and North Africa. It has become naturalized throughout North America.

How to Plant: Horehound is a hardy plant in zone 4 that prefers deep, well-drained, sandy soil and full sun. It may become invasive.

Horehound grows easily from seed or division in spring.

Uses: When your grandfather had a cold, he may have sucked on a horehound lozenge. The herb has been used for centuries to open clogged nasal passages and alleviate other symptoms associated with the sniffles. One of the Hebrew's ritual bitter herbs, horehound was also prized by the Greeks and Egyptians. Herbalists have employed it to treat hepatitis and jaundice. But horehound's most reliable uses are to soothe sore throats, help the lungs expel mucus, and treat bronchitis. A weak sedative, it also helps normalize an irregular heartbeat. It induces sweating and will lower a fever, especially when infused and drunk as a hot tea.

The herb's primary constituents include an essential oil, tannin, and a bitter chemical called marrubiin. The plant also contains vitamin C, which adds to its ability to fight colds. Horehound has a taste similar to sage and hyssop but more bitter. At one time it was used in England as a bitter to flavor ale.

Name: <u>Horseradish</u>

Botanical Name: *Armoracia rusticana*

Description: Horseradish, a cousin of mustard, produces a long tapering root. Its flowers are small and white and appear in midsummer; its leaves are abundant. Native to southeastern Europe and western Asia, the herb is cultivated widely in North America and naturalized in some areas.

How to Plant: Horseradish prefers average, moist, heavy soil and full sun. Once established, it is difficult to eradicate. Some gardeners believe that planting horseradish near potatoes makes them more disease-resistant.

Take cuttings 8 to 9 inches long from the root in the spring. Each cutting should have a bud. Place them 12 inches apart in soil that is at least 12 to 15 inches deep.

Uses: Have you ever bitten into a roast beef sandwich and thought your nose was on fire? The sandwich probably contained horseradish. Even a tiny taste of this potent condiment seems to go straight to your nose. Whether it's on a roast beef sandwich or in an herbal preparation, horseradish clears sinuses, increases circulation, and promotes expulsion of mucus from upper respiratory passages.

As a condiment, horseradish is widely used. Its sharp mustardy taste enhances mayonnaise, fish, beef, sausage, eggs, potatoes, and beets. Horseradish is used extensively in Eastern European cuisine and is a featured ingredient in Dresden sauce. Tender new leaves may be chopped fine and tossed in salads.

Name: <u>Horsetail</u>

Botanical Name: *Equisetum arvense*

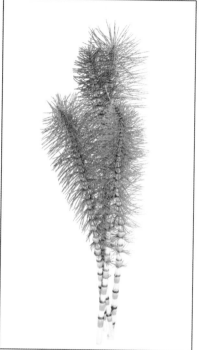

Description: One of the planet's oldest plant species, horsetail has been around for 200 million years. The herb's name refers to the resemblance of the whorls of its needlelike leaves to a horse's tail. The herb's other common name, scouring rush, derives from the plant's one-time use as a natural scouring pad for pots and pans. Horsetail appears in two stages: In the first, the herb produces a green-yellowish bamboolike stalk; in the second, whorls of threadlike leaves appear around the stalk. Harvest it in this second stage in the spring while it is still young. You'll likely encounter this herb in moist woods, along roads, and in waste places.

How to Plant: Horsetail prefers acidic to neutral, moist soil and partial shade. You can purchase horsetail at many nurseries. Once it has rooted, it's difficult to eradicate. Try planting the herb in a bucket placed just below the surface of a pond.

Horsetails are easy to divide. Dig and divide the roots.

Uses: Horsetail is high in minerals, particularly silica. The herb contains so much silica, in fact, that you can use it to polish metal. Early Americans used horsetail to scour pots and pans. Horsetail treats water retention, bed-wetting, and other bladder problems, including kidney stones. It is also used to decrease an enlarged prostate. Used externally, it stops bleeding and helps wounds to heal. It was once used to prevent the lungs from scarring in people with tuberculosis.

Because it contains minerals, horsetail strengthens bone, hair, and fingernails. Horsetail infusions—often combined with nettles—are drunk to help broken bones mend. The silica in it encourages the absorption of calcium by the body and helps prevent build-up of fatty deposits in the arteries.

Name: <u>Juniper</u>

Botanical Name: *Juniperus communis*

Description: Most junipers are low growing, with tangled, spreading branches covered with reddish-brown bark. The many varieties of juniper vary in size, color, and shape. Most cultivated junipers are dwarf varieties. The tree produces male and female flowers on separate plants. Juniper blooms from April through June and produces berries that ripen to a bluish-purple in the tree's second year. The berries are covered with a whitish wax, and its leaves are green, prickly, and needle-shaped.

How to Plant: Hardy trees, junipers will grow just about anywhere. They prefer full sun and sandy or light, loamy soil. To produce berries, you must grow both male and female plants. Once established, junipers require little care.

Sow seed in the spring or fall, but germination may take two to three years. In late summer, take cuttings, which root easily if kept moist. Seedlings, available at nurseries, may be transplanted at any time of year, although they do better in early spring or fall.

Uses: The berries give gin its distinct flavor. American Indians used the leaves and berries externally to cure infections, relieve arthritis, and treat wounds. Adding a handful of crushed juniper leaves to a warm bath soothes aching muscles.

Juniper's essential oils relieve coughs and lung congestion. Its tars and resins treat psoriasis and other skin conditions. In both treatments, juniper has a warming, circulation-stimulating action. Juniper also relieves gas in the digestive system, increases stomach acid, and is a diuretic.

Drink up to 1 cup of tea a day. Take the tea or tincture for one week, then abstain for one or two. Take 10 to 20 drops of tincture no more than four times a day. To make a massage oil, dilute juniper berry essential oil with vegetable oil. Rub on the skin over the urinary tract or digestive tract.

Name: <u>Lavender</u>

Botanical Name: *Lavandula angustifolia*

Description: Lavender is a bushy plant with silver-gray, narrow leaves. It produces abundant 1 1/2–2-foot flower stalks topped by fragrant and attractive purple-blue flower clusters. The plant flowers in June and July. An outstanding addition to any garden design, the herb also makes a nice edging or potted plant. There are a number of species and cultivars of lavender. Differences focus primarily on flower color (some have white, others, pink flowers), size, and growth habits.

How to Plant: Lavender prefers full sun in well-drained, sandy to poor, alkaline soil.

Sow seed in spring; take cuttings or layer before the plant flowers.

Uses: Perhaps the smell of lavender reminds you of soap. That's because lavender is a prime ingredient of many soaps. Its name, in fact, derives from the Latin "to wash." The Romans and Greeks used lavender in the bath. Lavender is also found commercially in shaving creams, colognes, and perfumes. It is used in many cosmetics and aromatherapy products because it is so versatile, and its fragrance blends so well with other herbs. Studies show that the scent is very relaxing. Lavender's scent is also a remedy for headache and nervous tension.

Lavender cosmetics are good for all complexion types. It is an excellent skin healer: It promotes the healing of burns, abrasions, infected sores, and other types of inflammations, including varicose veins. It is also a popular hair rinse. The herb is a carminative (relieves gas and bowel pain) and antispasmodic. It is most often used for sore muscles in the form of a massage oil. As recently as World War I, lavender was used in the field as a disinfectant for wounds; herbalists still recommend it for that purpose. Lavender destroys several viruses, including many that cause colds and flu. It also relieves lung and sinus congestion. Lavender flowers may be added to vinegars, jellies, sachets, and potpourri. Place a sprig of lavender in a drawer to freshen linens. And dried flowers make wonderful herbal arrangements, although they are fragile.

Name: <u>Lemon Balm</u>

Botanical Name: *Melissa officinalis*

Description: Lemon balm is an attractive plant with shield-shaped leaves that smell strongly of lemon. Like most mints, the herb produces square stems and flowers from July through September. Lemon balm is native to Europe and North Africa but has become naturalized elsewhere, including many parts of the United States.

How to Plant: Lemon balm prospers in full sun but will also do well in partial shade. It likes a well-drained or moist, sandy soil. The plant grows abundantly. It attracts honey-bees but repels other insects. Lemon balm is susceptible to developing powdery mildew, so avoid overhead watering if this is a problem. It is susceptible to frost and may need to be mulched during the winter in a cold climate.

Sow seeds or divide in autumn or early spring; take cuttings in spring and summer. However, lemon balm self-seeds so profusely, you may need only to transplant it once after it is established.

Uses: This venerable herb has been used for at least 2,000 years. Homer mentions the balm in his epic Odyssey. And Greek and Roman physicians prescribed it to treat injuries from scorpions and dogs. Colonists brought lemon balm to America. Thomas Jefferson grew it at Monticello, and many Old Williamsburg recipes call for its use.

Researchers have found that a mixture of lemon balm and valerian is as effective as some tranquilizers, without the side effects. The scent alone has long been used to reduce nervous tension. Compounds in it may even prove useful to people with hyper-thyroidism, although the herb itself won't replace thyroid medication. And its essential oil reduces risk of infections by inhibiting growth of bacteria and viruses.

In the kitchen, this herb, with its lemony-mint flavor, complements salads, fruits, marinated vegetables, poultry and stuffing, punch, fish marinades, and an assortment of vegetables, including corn, broccoli, asparagus, and beans. Lemon balm infusions cleanse the skin and help clear up acne.

Name: <u>Licorice</u>

Botanical Name: *Glycyrrhiza glabra*

Description: Licorice sends out stolons that create a tangled mass of taproots. The herb flowers in midsummer; in climates with a long growing season, the herb produces a fruit pod clustered in a prickly pod.

How to Plant: Licorice prefers neutral, well-drained, sandy soil and full sun to partial shade. In cold climates, take the plants inside during the winter. Licorice will handle only a light frost.

Sow seed in early spring or late fall; take cuttings from suckers.

Uses: Licorice has been a popular flavoring for millennia. Archaeologists have determined that the Assyrians and Egyptians used it. Licorice's main constituent, glycyrrhizin, is 50 times sweeter than sugar. Although the herb was once a popular candy flavoring, most of the licorice candy made in the United States is actually flavored with anise.

Like the adrenal hormone cortisone, it decreases inflammation, so it is used to reduce the symptoms of rheumatoid arthritis and other inflammatory disorders but without cortisone's side effects. And while cortisone therapy depletes the adrenal glands, licorice encourages them to function better and relieves adrenal exhaustion.

Take licorice in the form of syrup, tea, tincture, or pills. Use no more than 1 cup of tea or 1/8 teaspoon (1/2 dropper full) of tincture a day. You can also chew on the dried roots.

Name: <u>Marjoram</u>

Botanical Name: *Origanum majorana* or *Majorana hortensis*

Description: Marjoram is a bushy, spreading, fairly hardy perennial that is grown as an annual in freezing climates. It produces small, oval, gray-green, velvety leaves and knotlike shapes that blossom into tiny white or pink flowers from August through September. The herb makes an attractive potted plant that may be brought inside when temperatures fall. Native to southwest Asia, marjoram has become naturalized in Mediterranean regions and is cultivated widely in North America.

How to Plant: Like its cousin oregano (*Origanum vulgare*), marjoram likes average to sandy, well-drained alkaline soil and full sun. If your winters are severe, grow marjoram as an annual or in pots that may be brought indoors. If you keep it outdoors, shelter it from the cold.

Sow seed indoors a few weeks before the last frost and transplant outdoors after the soil has warmed; take cuttings in spring.

Uses: The Greeks knew marjoram as "joy of the mountains" and used it as a remedy for sadness. Herbalists have prescribed marjoram to treat asthma, increase sweating, lower fevers, encourage menstruation, and, especially, relieve indigestion. European singers preserved their voices with marjoram tea sweetened with honey. The herb has antioxidant and antifungal properties.

An infusion added to the bath helps relieve aches, pains, and congestion. Marjoram's antiseptic properties make it a good facial cleanser, and it has been used in cosmetic facial waters. Marjoram freshens linen drawers, and you can add it to potpourri and sachets. Dried flowers may be used in crafts and arrangements.

Marjoram can be made into tea, but by far, the most common way to use it is in cooking. It is also available as an essential oil that can be diluted in vegetable oil and applied to the skin. A couple drops of essential oil can be added to a bath or steam.

Name: <u>Milk Thistle</u>

Botanical Name: *Silybum marianum*

Description: Milk thistle leaves are large, shiny, and spiny. Violet-purple flowers appear from late summer to early autumn. Milk thistle is native to central and western Europe and has become naturalized elsewhere. It is often found on dry, rocky or stony soils in wastelands and fields, and along roads.

How to Plant: Milk thistle prefers sun and well-drained soil.

The herb grows easily from seed.

Uses: Legend has it that milk thistle sprang from the milk of the Virgin Mary, and for centuries, herbalists have recommended it for increasing milk in nursing mothers. But the herb's primary use in modern times is in detoxifying and nourishing the liver. The flavonoids in milk thistle repair damaged liver cells, stimulate production of new cells, and protect existing cells. In Europe, victims of Amanita mushroom poisoning who received preparations made from a compound in milk thistle survived. This is remarkable because Amanita mushrooms are normally considered deadly—most people who eat them die of liver failure. Herbalists prescribe milk thistle to treat jaundice, hepatitis, cirrhosis, and other liver conditions caused by alcohol abuse.

Milk thistle contains essential oils, tyramine, histamine, and a flavonoid called silymarine. Milk thistle has antioxidant properties and counteracts some of the detrimental effects of environmental toxins. A bitter tonic, the leaves stimulate bile production—it has been prescribed to improve appetite and assist digestion. Once cultivated widely as a nutritious culinary herb, young milk thistle leaves may be eaten as a salad or potherb. To eat the leaves, cut off their sharp edges with scissors and steam. Serve as you would spinach.

Name: <u>Nettle</u>

Botanical Name: *Urtica dioica*

Description: Brush against a bushy nettle plant and you'll feel as if you've been stung by bees. The herb's single stalk forms dark-green, saw-toothed leaves, which are covered with tiny "hairs" containing formic acid, a substance that causes pain if it comes in contact with your skin. Nettle's small, greenish flowers appear in clusters from July through September. The herb is native to Europe and Asia and widely naturalized.

How to Plant: Nettle prefers average to rich, moist soil and full sun to partial shade. Gardeners like it in their gardens because nettle may stimulate growth and production of essential oils in companion plants. Nettle also hosts several beneficial insects that prey on harmful pests. But it can be very invasive. To prevent this, cut it way back when harvesting before it goes to seed. You may need to do this several times every summer.

Nettle grows from seeds dispersed in spring, or you can produce new plants by dividing in spring or fall.

Uses: Nettle was once used to reduce arthritic pains and uric acid in joints and tissues (excess uric acid causes gout, a painful inflammatory condition). Nettle improves circulation and treats asthma. It is a light laxative; nettle tea has also been prescribed for intestinal weakness, diarrhea, and malnutrition. Nettle is a diuretic useful for treating bladder problems. Nettle treats eczema and skin rashes, increases mother's milk, slightly lowers blood sugar, and decreases profuse menstruation.

Nettle is so versatile that it has been used for centuries as a spring tonic to improve general health. The herb is rich in flavonoids and vital nutrients, including vitamins D, C, and A as well as minerals, such as iron, calcium, phosphorus, and magnesium. Thus, nettle has been used to treat malnutrition, anemia, and rickets. Hair shampoos and conditioners often include nettle because it is said to benefit the scalp and encourage hair growth.

Name: <u>Oats</u>

Botanical Name: *Avena sativa*

Description: The grass produces a fibrous root and a hollow jointed stem with narrow, flat, pale-green leaves. The grain is "hairy" and grooved. Oats are native to southern Europe and eastern Asia. They are widely cultivated as a food.

How to Plant: Widely cultivated for their nourishing grain, oats can also be grown in an herb garden.

Sow seed in spring.

Uses: The oat seed is used in two different phases of its growth: in its fresh, milky stage and as a grain once the seed is ripe and dried. In its milky stage, oat tincture has been prescribed for nerve disorders and as a uterine tonic. Researchers found that fresh oats have some value in treating addiction and reducing nicotine craving. Fresh, green oats ease the anxiety that often accompanies drug withdrawal. Oat straw is sometimes made into a high-mineral tea.

Oatmeal has been used topically to heal wounds and various skin rashes. With their demulcent and soothing qualities, oats are found in soaps and bath and body products. Oatmeal baths and poultices are wonderful for soothing dry, flaky skin or alleviating itching from poison oak and chicken pox. Used in the bath, oatmeal makes a good facial scrub and helps clear up skin problems.

Take 1/4 to 3/4 teaspoon (1 to 3 droppers full) a day of a tincture of fresh oats. Make a paste by adding water to ground oats. You can easily grind them in a coffee grinder or a food processor.

Name: <u>Parsley</u>

Botanical Name: *Petroselinum crispum*

Description: Parsley is often grown as an annual to obtain fresh-tasting leaves. The herb's attractive, rich-green, dense leaves form a rosette base, and the plant produces tiny, greenish-yellow flowers in early summer. Parsley comes in two forms: curly and Italian. The latter has flat leaves and is stronger-flavored than the curly variety. Curly parsley makes a nice edging plant, and both varieties can be grown in pots indoors. Parsley grows wild in many parts of the world and is cultivated throughout the temperate world.

How to Plant: Parsley prefers full sun or partial shade in a moist, rich soil. Parsley is said to repel asparagus beetles.

Soak seeds in warm water for several hours to speed germination. Sow seeds in the garden once the soil is warm in spring. The seeds often take many weeks to germinate. Parsley is difficult to transplant unless small.

Uses: You may think of parsley as a "throw-away" herb. It is universally used as a garnish that often goes uneaten. But if you discard this natural breath sweetener, you'll be wasting a powerhouse of vitamins and minerals. Parsley contains vitamins A and C (more than an orange), and small amounts of several B vitamins, calcium, and iron.

Parsley seeds, or a compound in them, is used in some pharmaceutical preparations to treat urinary tract disorders. Another of parsley's compounds reduces inflammation and is a free radical scavenger, eliminating these destructive elements. It also stimulates the appetite and increases circulation to the digestive organs. The root has more medicinal properties than the leaves.

Parsley's clean flavor blends with most foods and is often found in ethnic cuisines, including those of the Middle East, France, Belgium, Switzerland, Japan, Spain, and England. Parsley complements most meats and poultry and is a good addition to vegetable dishes, soups, and stews.

Name: <u>Passion Flower</u>

Botanical Name: *Passiflora incarnata*

Description: Passion flower produces coiling tendrils and showy, colorful blossoms with white or lavender petals and a brilliant pink or purple corona. Flowers appear from early to late summer. The plant produces three to five toothed, lobed leaves and a berry with thin yellow skin and a sweet, succulent pulp. Passion flower is native from Florida to Texas and may be found as far north as Missouri. The herb also is abundant in South America. Passion flower grows in full sun to partially shaded, dry areas, in thickets, along fences, and at the edge of wooded areas.

How to Plant: Passion flower prefers deep, well-drained soil, plenty of water, and some shade. Revitalize the soil each spring, replacing the top layer with new topsoil, but don't over-fertilize since very rich soil results in fewer flowers. Prune old branches in late winter and early spring to get better blossoms. You can also grow passion flower indoors in a large pot, although it won't reach its normal height.

Sow seeds in the spring, although they can take years to germinate. Take cuttings in spring or fall. Plants are sold in most nurseries.

Uses: Few herbs have as many religious connections as passion flower. When Spanish explorers discovered the vine growing in South America, they were struck by its elaborate blossoms. Passion flower's five petals and five sepals, they reasoned, represented the 10 faithful apostles. The flower's dramatic corona looked to them like Jesus's crown of thorns. And the herb's five stamens symbolized Christ's five wounds.

Passion flower's chief medicinal value is as a sedative. The Aztecs used it to promote sleep and relieve pain. Today the flowers are used in numerous pharmaceutical drugs in Europe to treat nervous disorders, heart palpitations, anxiety, and high blood pressure. It has also been prescribed for tension, fatigue, insomnia, and muscle and lung spasms. Unlike most sedative drugs, it has been shown to be nonaddictive, although it is not a strong pain reliever.

Name: <u>Peppermint</u>

Botanical Name: *Mentha piperita*

Description: Peppermint produces dark-green, spear-shaped leaves on stems that arise from an underground network of spreading stems. Though peppermint and spearmint are close relatives, spearmint (*M. spicata*) has green, pointed, somewhat hairy leaves and has a milder, cooler taste. Both plants can become invasive, so plant them in an isolated location, or contain the herbs in a pot. The herb flowers in July and August. Mints are native to Europe and Asia; some varieties are found in South Africa, America, and Australia.

How to Plant: Peppermint likes full sun to partial shade and average, moist soil. Mints are said to repel aphids, flea beetles, and cabbage pests.

Take cuttings in midsummer; divide at any time during the growing season.

Uses: You may enjoy peppermint candies, especially after a meal, but this useful plant isn't found just in confections. A carminative and gastric stimulant, promoting the flow of bile to the stomach and aiding digestion, peppermint has been prescribed to treat indigestion, flatulence, colic, and nausea. An antispasmodic, peppermint calms muscles in the digestive tract, reduces colon spasms, and is recommended as a treatment for irritable bowel syndrome and colitis.

Peppermint is used to flavor candy, gum, and even dental products and toothpicks. Peppermint makes a good addition to sachets and potpourri. Sniffing peppermint helps clear the sinuses, so it is often used in inhalers.

Name: <u>Red Clover</u>

Botanical Name: *Trifolium pratense*

Description: This wide-ranging legume produces leaves in groups of three and fragrant red or purple ball-shaped flowers. Like its relatives, beans and peas, red clover adds nitrogen to the soil. Sufficient nitrogen is important to produce healthy plants. As a result, red clover is a popular winter and early spring cover crop to enrich the soil, but because it is a tenacious perennial that spreads by means of runners, it must be well chopped before you replant the garden. You'll find it growing in fields and vacant lots. The plant is widely cultivated.

How to Plant: Red clover thrives in moist, well-drained soil with full sun.

Sow seeds in the spring or fall.

Uses: Red clover, a favorite of honey bees, is one of the world's oldest agricultural crops. This ubiquitous field flower has been used as a medicine for millennia, revered by Greeks, Romans, and Celts. But it's in the last 100 years that red clover has gained prominence as the source of a possible cancer treatment. Researchers have isolated several antitumor compounds such as biochanin A in red clover, which they think may help prevent cancer. The herb also contains antioxidants and a form of vitamin E.

Some of red clover's constituents are thought to stimulate the immune system. Another constituent, coumarin, has blood-thinning properties. Its hormone-mimicking effect makes red clover a potential treatment for some types of infertility and symptoms of menopause. A diuretic, sedative, and anti-inflammatory herb, red clover has been recommended for the skin conditions eczema and psoriasis. It also has some anti-bacterial properties.

You may pick flowers and add them to salads throughout the summer. Tiny florets are a delightful addition to iced tea. Eat red clover's nutritious leaves cooked since they are not digestible raw.

Name: Rosemary

Botanical Name: *Rosmarinus officinalis*

Description: Rosemary makes a stunning addition to any garden. An attractive, spreading evergreen, its gray-green, needle-shaped leaves may be pruned to form a low hedge. A low-growing variety of rosemary provides a wonderful ground cover. The herb produces pale blue flowers from December through spring. Rosemary is found on hills along the Mediterranean, in Portugal, and in northwestern Spain. The herb is cultivated widely elsewhere.

How to Plant: Rosemary likes sandy, alkaline soil and full sun but will grow in partial sun. Grow rosemary as a potted plant in cold climates, or protect it from winter winds.

Sow seed; take cuttings or layer in spring.

Uses: Before the advent of refrigeration, cooks wrapped meat in rosemary leaves to preserve it. The herb's strong piney aroma has prevented commercial use as a preservative, but efforts are underway to create a preservative without the scent. Modern studies show that rosemary has potent antioxidant properties. It is an astringent, expectorant, and diaphoretic (induces sweating). It promotes digestion and stimulates the activity of the liver and gallbladder to aid both in digestion of fats and the detoxification of the body. It also inhibits formation of kidney stones.

In the kitchen, rosemary's pungent taste—something like mint and ginger—complements poultry, fish, lamb, beef, veal, pork, game, cheese, and eggs, as well as many vegetables, including potatoes, tomatoes, spinach, peas, and mushrooms. Rosemary essential oil is found in soaps, creams, lotions, and perfumes. The oil and herb are added to cosmetics to improve skin tone.

Name: <u>Sage</u>

Botanical Name: *Salvia officinalis*

Description: Sage produces long, oval, gray-green, slightly textured leaves; it comes in variegated and purple-leaved varieties. Sage is a good edging plant, attractive in any garden. In June, the herb produces whorls of pink, purple, blue, or white flowers. Sage is native to the Mediterranean. A hardy plant, it has become naturalized elsewhere and is cultivated as far north as Canada.

How to Plant: Sage prefers full sun in a well-drained, sandy, alkaline soil. Protect it from the wind. Sage is said to enhance growth of cabbages, carrots, strawberries, and tomatoes, but some gardeners recommend that you keep it away from onions.

Sow seed, take cuttings, divide, or layer in spring.

Uses: You may associate sage with Thanksgiving. The herb is often used to flavor poultry dressings. The Arabs associated sage with immortality, and the Greeks considered it an herb that promotes wisdom. Appropriately enough, a constituent in sage was recently discovered to inhibit an enzyme that produces memory loss and plays a role in Alzheimer disease. However, it's unlikely that use of the herb alone will benefit these conditions. Sage's essential oils have antiseptic properties, and the tannins are astringent. It has been used for centuries as a gargle for sore throat and inflamed gums. The herb is useful in treating mouth sores, cuts, and bruises.

Sage's sharp, almost camphorlike taste complements salads, egg dishes, soups, breads, marinades, sausage, beef, pork, veal, fish, lamb, duck, goose, and a variety of vegetables, including tomatoes, asparagus, beans, and onions.

Name: St. John's Wort

Botanical Name: *Hypericum perforatum*

Description: The bright yellow flowers of this erect herb appear from June to July. Green leaves are small and oblong and appear to have "pores" when held up to the light. Native to Europe, St. John's wort has become naturalized throughout North America in woods and meadows. St. John's wort received its name perhaps because it blooms around June 24, the day celebrated as the birthday of Christ's cousin, John the Baptist. The herb exudes a reddish oil from its glands when a leaf is crushed.

How to Plant: St. John's wort is a wild herb that may be transplanted to a garden. A hardy herb, it will grow in most soils.

Sow seed in spring.

Uses: St. John's wort has been used as a medicine for centuries. Early European and Slavic herbals mention it. It has long been used as an anti-inflammatory for bruises, varicose veins, hemorrhoids, strains, sprains, and contusions. It is used internally and topically (in tincture, oil, or salve form) for these conditions. The plant, especially its flowers, is high in flavonoid compounds that reduce inflammation.

Studies show that St. John's wort relieves anxiety and is an antidepressant. Some researchers believe that one of its constituents, hypericin, interferes with the body's production of a depression-related chemical called monoamine oxidase (MAO).

The herb has also been used to treat skin problems, urinary conditions such as bed-wetting, painful nerve conditions such as carpal tunnel syndrome, and symptoms of nerve destruction.

Take 1/2 to 1 teaspoon (2 to 4 droppers full) of tincture up to three times a day. You can take St. John's wort pills, but be sure they are made from either freeze-dried herbs or a dried extract since the herb loses most of its medicinal properties when air-dried.

186

Name: Skullcap

Botanical Name: *Scutellaria lateriflora*

Description: Skullcap is a slender, branching, square-stemmed plant with opposite, serrated leaves. Its blue flowers, which have two "lips," resemble the skullcaps worn in medieval times, hence, the herb's name. Several species of skullcap grow in Europe and Asia. Also known as mad dog weed and Virginia skullcap, the herb is found in the United States and southern Canada.

How to Plant: Skullcap prefers well-drained, moist soil and partial shade. Once rooted, the herb requires little care.

Sow seeds or divide roots in early spring. Thin seedlings to 6 inches.

Uses: Skullcap received its common name, mad dog weed, in the 18th century, when the herb was widely prescribed as a cure for rabies, although no scientific evidence supports its use for that disease. The herb is a sedative often recommended for treating insomnia, nervousness, nervous twitches, and anxiety. Russian researchers have found that skullcap helps stabilize stress-related heart disease. Skullcap has been found to have anti-inflammatory properties.

Take skullcap as a tea, a tincture, or in pills. The taste is slightly bitter, so most people mix it with peppermint or chamomile when they drink it as a tea. In formulas to ease nervous system problems, it is mixed with herbs such as valerian, passion flower, and chamomile. Take up to 2 cups of tea or 1/2 teaspoon (2 droppers full) of tincture a day.

Name: <u>Tarragon</u>

Botanical Name: *Artemisia dracunculus*

Description: This perennial has long, narrow, pointed leaves, but its flowers rarely appear. Be sure to get the French rather than the Russian variety of tarragon. The Russian variety looks much the same but has somewhat narrower, lighter green leaves, and it flowers and produces seed. But Russian tarragon has less of the sweetly aromatic flavor of its French cousin. Test the plant by crushing, smelling, and tasting a few leaves. Tarragon is probably native to the Caspian Sea area and possibly Siberia and Europe. It is cultivated in Europe, Asia, and the United States.

How to Plant: Tarragon prefers full sun to partial shade in a sandy, average, well-drained alkaline soil. It may also be grown successfully as a potted plant. Cut tarragon back in the fall or early spring. Protect it with mulch during winter. Tarragon is said to enhance the growth of most companion vegetables.

Since it produces no seeds, buy your first plant, then take cuttings in summer and fall; divide or layer in early spring.

Uses: Thomas Jefferson was one of the first Americans to grow this lovely and useful plant. Tarragon stimulates appetite, relieves gas and colic, and makes a good local anesthetic for toothaches. Tarragon has anti-fungal and antioxidant properties and has been used to preserve foods. It's also found in perfumes, soaps, cosmetics, condiments, and liqueurs. One of the French fines herbs, tarragon has a strong flavor that may over-power foods, so use it sparingly in salads and sauces, including remoulade, tartar, and béarnaise sauces.

Name: <u>Thyme</u>

Botanical Name: *Thymus vulgaris*

Description: These tiny-leaved, wide-spreading perennials make a good inexpensive ground cover that can be clipped and mowed regularly. Thyme's profuse lilac to pink blooms appear in June and July and are especially attractive to bees. There are many species and varieties of thyme with self-descriptive names, including woolly thyme, silver thyme, lemon thyme, and golden thyme.

How to Plant: Thyme does well in full sun in poor to average, well-drained soil. Trim it back each spring to encourage abundant new growth. It also may be grown as a potted plant. Some gardeners believe that thyme enhances growth of eggplant, potatoes, and tomatoes. It is said to repel cabbage worms and whiteflies.

Sow seed or divide in spring or fall; take cuttings or layer in early summer.

Uses: You may have noticed thyme's distinctive flavor in cough medicines. Thymol, a prime constituent, is found in a number of them. Thymol is also used commercially to make colognes, aftershaves, lotions, soaps, detergents, and cosmetics. Thyme was used as an antiseptic to treat wounds as recently as World War I. In fact, it is one of the most potent antiseptics of all the herbs.

One of the French fines herbs, thyme complements salads, veal, lamb, beef, poultry, fish, stuffing, sausage, stews, soups, bread, butters, mayonnaise, vinegars, mustard, eggs, cheese, and many vegetables, including tomatoes, onions, eggplant, leeks, mushrooms, asparagus, and green beans.

Name: <u>Valerian</u>

Botanical Name: *Valeriana officinalis*

Description: There are some 200 species of valerian, a plant with an erect, hollow, hairy stem that produces four to eight pairs of dark green leaves. Held on tall, thin stalks, valerian flowers are small and pink-tinged and appear in June through July. Various medicinal species of the herb are native to Europe and western Asia and grow wild in North America. There are also several native American species.

How to Plant: Valerian prefers rich, moist soil and full sun to partial shade.

Divide roots in spring or fall. Seeds germinate poorly. Sow them in a cold frame in April and transplant in May. Divide valerian every three years to prevent overcrowding.

Uses: Ask most people what the smell of valerian reminds them of and they're likely to say old socks. Nonetheless, cats go wild over valerian and so do rats. Lore has it, in fact, that the Pied Piper used valerian to rid Hameln of rodents. In ancient times, valerian was widely used as a treatment for epilepsy. Today valerian finds its chief value in soothing anxiety and promoting sleep.

The relaxing action of valerian also makes it useful for treatment of muscle cramps, menstrual cramps, and high blood pressure. Valerian relaxes vein and artery walls and is especially indicated for blood pressure elevations caused by stress and worry. Valerian is recommended for tension headaches as well as heart palpitations.

Valerian mildly stimulates the intestines, can help dispel gas and cramps in the digestive tract, and is weakly antimicrobial, particularly to bacteria. Valerian improves stomach function and relieves gas and painful bowel spasms.

Name: Yarrow

Botanical Name: *Achillea millefolium*

Description: Yarrow's Latin name means "a thousand leaves," a reference to the herb's fine, feathery foliage. Erect and covered with silky "hairs," yarrow produces white flower heads from June through September. The herb is native to Europe but has become naturalized throughout North America. You'll find yarrow growing along roads and in fields and waste places.

How to Plant: Yarrow likes full sun and well-drained soil. The herb will adapt to almost any type of garden except those with soggy soil. Creeping species of yarrow, which may be mowed, will rot unless the soil is well drained. Occasionally, yarrow falls prey to powdery mildew, rust, or stem rot. Yarrow may benefit companion plants by attracting helpful insects, such as wasps and lady bugs.

Sow seed in the spring; divide in spring or fall.

Uses: In the epic *Iliad*, Homer reports that legendary warrior Achilles used yarrow leaves to treat the wounds of his fallen comrades. Studies show that yarrow is a fine herb indeed for accelerating healing of cuts and bruises. The Greeks used the herb to stop hemorrhages. Gerard's famous herbal cited yarrow's benefits in 1597. And after colonists brought the plant to America, Native Americans used it to treat bleeding, wounds, infections, headaches, indigestion, and sore throat.

Clinical studies have supported the long-standing use of yarrow to cleanse wounds and make blood clot faster. Yarrow treats bleeding stomach ulcers, heavy menstrual periods, and bleeding from the bowels. An essential oil known as azulene is responsible for yarrow's ability to reduce inflammation.

The herb also contains salicylic acid, aspirin's main constituent, making it useful for relieving pain. Chewing the leaves or root is an old toothache remedy. Yarrow fights bacteria and dries up congestion in sinus and other respiratory infections and allergies.

Name: <u>Yellow Dock</u>

Botanical Name: *Rumex crispus*

Description: Yellow dock produces a yellow taproot, leaves that taper to a point, and whorls of greenish flowers that appear on tall stems in mid-summer. The herb is native to Eurasia and grows as a weed throughout temperate and subtropical regions.

How to Plant: Yellow dock is a wild plant that likes poor to average soil in weedy places.

Plants grow from seed in spring.

Uses: Yellow dock root stimulates intestinal secretions and promotes bile flow, which aids fat digestion and has a light laxative action. The root is also used to treat anemia and can dramatically increase iron levels in the blood in only a few weeks. Long considered a blood purifier, yellow dock may also be effective in treating a number of conditions that stem from liver dysfunction, including skin eruptions, headaches, and unhealthy hair and nails. An astringent and tonic, yellow dock has been used to treat ringworm, laryngitis, and gingivitis.

Steam or sauté very young leaves as you would greens. The tall flower stalks are used in dried flower arrangements and are prized by flower arrangers because they retain their attractive rusty-red color when dried.

You can drink up to 3 to 4 cups a day of yellow dock tea. However, yellow dock is bitter, so add herbs such as peppermint or lemon balm to improve the flavor.